5 Minutes with Jesus

Peace for Today

Sheila Walsh

THOMAS NELSON
Since 1798

Published in Nashville, Tennessee, by Thomas Nelson. Thomas Nelson is a registered trademark of HarperCollins Christian Publishing, Inc.

Special thanks to Sherri Gragg for her invaluable contribution to creating this book.

Cover design by Katie Jennings Design

Unless otherwise noted, Scripture quotations are taken from the ESV® Bible (The Holy Bible, English Standard Version®). Copyright © 2001 by Crossway, a publishing ministry of Good News Publishers. Used by permission. All rights reserved. Scripture quotations marked HCSB are taken from the Holman Christian Standard Bible®. Copyright © 1999, 2000, 2002, 2003, 2009 by Holman Bible Publishers. Used by permission. HCSB® is a federally registered trademark of Holman Bible Publishers. Scripture quotations marked THE MESSAGE are taken from *The Message.* Copyright © by Eugene H. Peterson 1993, 1994, 1995, 1996, 2000, 2001, 2002. Used by permission of Tyndale House Publishers, Inc. Scripture quotations marked NASB are taken from the New American Standard Bible®. Copyright © 1960, 1962, 1963, 1968, 1971, 1972, 1973, 1975, 1977, 1995 by The Lockman Foundation. Used by permission. Scripture quotations marked NIV are taken from the Holy Bible, New International Version®, NIV®. Copyright © 1973, 1978, 1984, 2011 by Biblica, Inc.™ Used by permission of Zondervan. All rights reserved worldwide. www.zondervan. com. The "NIV" and "New International Version" are trademarks registered in the United States Patent and Trademark Office by Biblica, Inc.™ Scripture quotations marked NKJV are taken from the New King James Version®. © 1982 by Thomas Nelson. Used by permission. All rights reserved. Scripture quotations marked NLT are taken from the *Holy Bible*, New Living Translation. © 1996, 2004, 2007, 2013 by Tyndale House Foundation. Used by permission of Tyndale House Publishers, Inc., Carol Stream, Illinois 60188. All rights reserved.

Italicized text in Scripture quotations indicate the author's emphasis.

ISBN-13: 978-0-7180-3255-5

Printed in China

16 17 18 19 20 DSC 6 5 4 3 2 1

Introduction

W hat did you do to get us to fall asleep?" Kate texted her mom.

Kate was nineteen and a pretty experienced baby-sitter, but ready to retire from that gig after trying for forty-five minutes to get Kyle to wind down and fall asleep.

Her mother reminisced: "When you were tiny, I would give you a gentle *pat-pat*, *pat-pat* on the back, or I'd softly sing 'Amazing Grace' and 'When I Survey the Wondrous Cross.' Sometimes we rocked in the rocking chair. You liked having your back scratched with a big comb! But of course there were times when I thought you were asleep, and I'd quietly tiptoe out of the room . . . then you made it clear that you definitely weren't asleep!"

Even little people—who have only food, diapers, and hugs as their major concerns—can have trouble finding peace when it's time to sleep. We not-so-little people have a much longer list of concerns that rob us of peace.

In fact, Jesus promised us that we'd have a list! He was very straightforward: "Here on earth you will have many trials and sorrows" (John 16:33 NLT). This world hasn't disappointed, has it? Among the many external peace-robbers are children to raise, jobs to maintain, deadlines to meet, bills to pay, chores to do, friends to support. And each of us has internal peace-robbers like fear, bitterness, exhaustion, or scars from long ago.

Jesus, however, did not just promise trials and sorrows. He also promised peace. Before His crucifixion, He told His disciples the troubling details "so that [they] may have peace" (v. 33 NLT). Events would appear out of control, but they were part of God's sovereign plan unfolding. When Jesus promised to send the Holy Spirit to His followers, He added, "I am leaving you with a gift—peace of mind and heart. And the peace I give is a gift the world cannot give. So don't be troubled or afraid" (John 14:27 NLT).

Jesus wants us to know peace, to receive the gift of peace He has for us, to live with "peace of mind and heart." Key to knowing Jesus' peace is spending time in His Word, and I pray this little book will help.

Whether I start a devotional by sharing a brief story or some thoughts on a Bible passage, I always end with a handful of Scripture passages. Even just making time to read through those verses will give you a moment of peace, but I'm confident that the truths you encounter in those words—the God you encounter as you read His words—will help you experience His peace after you close the book and continue through your day.

I want you to know I'd be thrilled to hear how spending time with Jesus is changing your life—and to cheer you on! In fact, I'm not the only one. There are many of us who want to remind each other that just five minutes a day can transform our entire lives. I joyfully welcome you into the supportive community we've been building at 5MinuteswithJesus.com, where you'll find inspiring images and videos and all kinds of encouragement.

Okay, so you've read about three pages. It may be time to get back to whatever might be your peace-robber! But go in peace . . . guided by your Good Shepherd. Remember to breathe deeply—and when you do, may that refreshing breath prompt from your heart a prayer to your Prince of Peace.

Peace be with you.
Sheila

Knowing Where to Look

I am not a natural athlete. To be more accurate, I am not any kind of athlete. And that became uncomfortably clear the first time I went skiing with my family.

Although Christian was only ten, he took to it immediately. I, however, spent the first two days on the bunny slopes—and I would have happily stayed there the whole week if my pesky instructor hadn't insisted that I was ready to move up.

Now I had imagined that the ski lift would be like an elevator: it would stop, the door would open, and I'd have a good ten minutes to get on. Not even close! It was a continuously moving row of seats that didn't stop—the lift barely slowed down—and I had to shuffle like a geriatric wiener dog to line up and then sit down. All I could hear in the background was my son calling out, "Mom, don't look down!"

Peter could have used such advice.

Matthew 14 tells us about a truly terrifying moment for the disciples when they looked up from their wind-buffeted boat in the dark of night to see a figure gliding across the water toward them. They thought it was a ghost! Scripture tells us they "cried out in fear" (v. 26). Jesus quickly identified Himself (the disciples were not seeing a ghost!) and let them know they were safe. When Peter heard this, he made a remarkable request: "Lord, if it is you, command me to come to you on the water" (v. 28). Jesus simply responded, "Come" (v. 29).

Peter gingerly slipped over the side of the boat and lowered his foot to the raging sea. It held firm! Then he looked toward Jesus and, step by wondrous step, began making his way toward the Savior.

If only Peter had kept his eyes on Jesus! Instead, the fierce wind caught his attention, and as his gaze shifted from Jesus to the tempest that raged around him, Peter began sinking. In his terror, he cried out for Jesus to save him—and Jesus "immediately reached out his hand and took hold of him" (v. 31).

We are guaranteed moments in this life when the winds of adversity rise, when our boat seems way too small for so vast an ocean, and when we can't bail water fast enough to stay afloat. We gaze into the fearsome storm that rages all around us and realize we can't navigate it on our own.

In such moments, what can save the child of God? What will

bring her peace? Peace comes when we remember whom to call and where to look.

Is a storm raging in your life today? Don't look down. Instead, keep your eyes on Jesus.

> **When the storm is the fiercest,**
> **fix your gaze on Christ alone.**

❧ Five Minutes in the Word ☙

My eyes are toward you, O GOD, my Lord; in you
I seek refuge; leave me not defenseless!

Psalm 141:8

Since we are surrounded by so great a cloud of witnesses, let
us also lay aside every weight, and sin which clings so closely,
and let us run with endurance the race that is set before us,
looking to Jesus, the founder and perfecter of our faith, who for
the joy that was set before him endured the cross, despising the
shame, and is seated at the right hand of the throne of God.

Hebrews 12:1–2

"I am leaving you with a gift—peace of mind and heart. And the peace I give is a gift the world cannot give. So don't be troubled or afraid."

John 14:27 NLT

"I have told you all this so that you may have peace in me. Here on earth you will have many trials and sorrows. But take heart, because I have overcome the world."

John 16:33 NLT

"Fear not, for I have redeemed you; I have called you by name, you are mine. When you pass through the waters, I will be with you; and through the rivers, they shall not overwhelm you; when you walk through fire you shall not be burned, and the flame shall not consume you."

Isaiah 43:1–2

Sowing Seeds of Peace

Some of God's most faithful servants had shown up prepared to do the work of His kingdom. The field for their labors was a courtroom in Charleston, South Carolina. They came bearing seeds of peace that they would sow and then water with tears.

The young man being arraigned had admitted to taking the lives of the people they loved most in the world, an act he had hoped would begin a racial war.

But God had sent these servants to the courtroom armed with only one weapon—the only one they needed: the love of Christ.

The judge turned to the victims' family members and asked if they had anything to say before he made a decision about bond. One by one, each person addressed the young man who had taken so much from them: "I forgive you," and "May God have mercy on your soul." The moment was truly awe-inspiring.[1]

The wisdom of God doesn't look anything like the wisdom of the world, which advocates self-promotion and vengeance. When the world sows these seeds, a crop of division and hate results.

Scripture tells us that God's wisdom, however, "is first of all pure; then peace-loving, considerate, submissive, full of mercy and good fruit, impartial and sincere. Peacemakers who sow in peace reap a harvest of righteousness" (James 3:17–18 NIV).

I think the important thing to remember both from this verse and from the example of our brothers and sisters in Charleston is that joining God in the work of peace can be difficult and costly. Fulfilling our God-ordained roles as peacemakers requires action and often sacrifice on our part, but we can be confident that our labor is never in vain. God will honor it.

Psalm 126:5–6 says, "Those who sow with tears will reap with songs of joy. Those who go out weeping, carrying seed to sow, will return with songs of joy, carrying sheaves with them" (NIV).

When we join God as peacemakers, doing the difficult work of scattering seeds of peace in our sin-broken world, we have the beautiful hope that we will one day be singing with joy as we witness the harvest God produced in part because of our faithful service.

> *Followers of Jesus who sow in peace reap a harvest of righteousness.*

❧ Five Minutes in the Word ❧

God is not unjust; he will not forget your work and the love you have shown him as you have helped his people and continue to help them. We want each of you to show this same diligence to the very end, so that what you hope for may be fully realized. We do not want you to become lazy, but to imitate those who through faith and patience inherit what has been promised.

Hebrews 6:10–12 NIV

Bear with each other and forgive one another if any of you has a grievance against someone. Forgive as the Lord forgave you. And over all these virtues put on love, which binds them all together in perfect unity. Let the peace of Christ rule in your hearts, since as members of one body you were called to peace. And be thankful.

Colossians 3:13–15 NIV

Love is patient and kind. Love is not jealous or boastful or proud or rude. It does not demand its own way. It is not irritable, and it keeps no record of being wronged. It does not rejoice about injustice but rejoices whenever the truth wins out. Love never gives up, never loses faith, is always hopeful, and endures through every circumstance.

1 Corinthians 13:4–7 NLT

Those who are peacemakers will plant seeds of peace and reap a harvest of righteousness.

James 3:18 NLT

"Blessed are the peacemakers, for they shall be called sons of God."

Matthew 5:9

No One Prepared
Me for This!

When I think back to the forty (which felt more like 423) weeks of being pregnant with my son, I'm sure I must have purchased every single book on the market related to child-rearing.

How to Raise a Godly Child

How to Raise an Independent Son

How to Raise a Future Leader

In retrospect I think I should have written one: *I Should Have Slept More the First Forty Years!*

There's a lot of great material available to walk you through the different stages from baby to toddler and all the way through high school. But before any dust can settle on your child's high school diploma, you suddenly realize that nothing prepared you for the next season: for letting go.

Christian was accepted into Texas A&M for the fall of 2015. The pile of his going-to-college stuff got bigger and bigger as the stifling heat of summer intensified and The Day got closer. When it finally arrived, we packed as many boxes as we could into his car and the rest into the SUV we had rented for exactly this purpose, and we hit the road. It was 105 degrees when we arrived in College Station. I have never sweat as much in my life as I did that day when I carried sheets, towels, pots and pans, boxes of protein bars, and enough popcorn to fill a bus up three flights of stairs.

Finally, he was all settled in, and it was time for us to leave. I will never forget that moment. Christian walked us out to our car. He hugged me for a long time, then looked me in the eyes and said, "Thank you." He did the same with his dad, and then we watched him turn and walk into all that God has for his life. I cried all the way home.

There are so many stages in life that little can prepare you for:

The death of a spouse

The loss of a job

Your daughter getting married and moving across the country

Your darling, only son heading off to college just as you prayed he would, but you had no idea how much it would hurt.

Where is the peace Christ promises in those moments when there is nothing you can do but sit in your new reality? For me, peace comes after admitting to God that I'm not in a good place. Have you noticed, in Scripture, how often peace comes after a storm? The great news about God is that you don't have to pretend to be where you're not.

If you're mad, be mad . . . then receive His peace.

If you're sad, cry till you have no tears left . . . and then receive His peace.

> *Peace is not something we can lose,*
> *because Christ Himself is our peace.*

❧ Five Minutes in the Word ☙

[Jesus] got up, rebuked the wind and said to the waves, "Quiet! Be still!" Then the wind died down and it was completely calm.

Mark 4:39 NIV

"God blesses those who are poor and realize their need for him, for the Kingdom of Heaven is theirs."

Matthew 5:3 NLT

Dear brothers and sisters, when troubles of any kind come your way, consider it an opportunity for great joy. For you know that when your faith is tested, your endurance has a chance to grow.

James 1:2–3 NLT

You have kept count of my tossings; put my tears in your bottle. Are they not in your book?

Psalm 56:8

You Have Known the Distress of My Soul

It was like trying to fill a bucket that has a hole in it.

For twenty-five years she had weathered an emotionally abusive marriage. She had tried to help her husband, but she never could do enough or give enough. She had forgiven and forgiven, granted countless second chances, and patched her broken heart back together over and over again.

Then one day she found she couldn't go any further. At last, the two of them found themselves in the office of a very good therapist. During the many months she spent there, she learned a lot and healed a lot. Then, in one of her last sessions, the therapist admitted to her that a couple of times her husband had actually succeeded in causing the therapist to doubt himself. "If he can do that to me," the therapist said, "I can't even imagine what he does to you."

"In that moment," she said, "I broke down in tears because, for the first time ever, someone truly understood."

Knowing that someone truly understands the deepest wounds of our souls is a powerful source of healing. That heart connection speaks peace into the fiercest storm and is salve for the most wounded heart. Having such a connection with another human being is truly wonderful, but Psalm 31 reveals the even sweeter truth that God Himself knows and understands our most desperate sorrows.

Listen to the psalmist in verse 7: "I will rejoice and be glad in your steadfast love, because you have seen my affliction; you have known the distress of my soul." The Hebrew word translated *rejoice* here means, literally, "to spin around." And—I love this—the term *steadfast love* can be translated "merciful kindness." When we put it all together, the verse comes out like this: "I will spin for joy and be glad because of Your merciful kindness to me, because You have seen my affliction; You have known the anguish of my soul." The psalmist found great comfort in knowing that God understood his pain—and that the One who understood him was mighty to save. That is indeed a reason to spin for joy.

> *God sees you, knows you, loves you, and is mighty to save.*

✦ Five Minutes in the Word ✦

The Lord your God is in your midst, a mighty one who will save; he will rejoice over you with gladness; he will quiet you by his love; he will exult over you with loud singing.
Zephaniah 3:17

You keep track of all my sorrows. You have collected all my tears in your bottle. You have recorded each one in your book.
Psalm 56:8 NLT

In my distress I cried out to the Lord; yes, I prayed to my God for help. He heard me from his sanctuary; my cry to him reached his ears.
Psalm 18:6 NLT

The Lord is near to the brokenhearted and saves the crushed in spirit.
Psalm 34:18

The LORD bless you and keep you; the LORD make his face shine on you and be gracious to you; the LORD turn his face toward you and give you peace.

Numbers 6:24–26 NIV

Show Me Your Glory

M oses never really wanted the job. He tried to talk God into picking someone else to lead the people out of Egypt, but God didn't take no for an answer. So Moses did what God asked: Moses went to Egypt, dueled verbally with Pharaoh, and then led God's motley crew of followers out of slavery.

But now, in the middle of nowhere, God was fed up with the Israelites' insolence and was threatening to abandon ship! "The LORD said to Moses, 'Depart; go up from here. . . . But I will not go up among you, lest I consume you on the way, for you are a stiff-necked people'" (Exodus 33:1, 3).

And however dumbfounded he was initially, Moses had a response to God's resignation speech: "Look, you tell me, 'Lead this people,' but you don't let me know whom you're going to send with me. You tell me, 'I know you well and you are special to me.' If I am so special to you, let me in on your plans. . . . Don't forget, this is *your* people, your responsibility" (vv. 12–13 THE MESSAGE).

God relented: He assured Moses that He would indeed accompany Israel on her way, but Moses wasn't convinced and asked again. And again God promised Moses that, yes, He would go with His people. But apparently Moses had been pushed too close to the brink. He needed more reassurance than God had yet offered. "Please show me your glory," Moses asked the Almighty (v. 18).

You've undoubtedly experienced moments in your life—I know I have—when none of the usual comforts bring peace. We need something bigger, truer, surer. We need a fresh glimpse of the One who holds our world in the palm of His hand. Peace comes to us in those darkest of nights as we cry out, like Moses, "Show me Your glory!"

Have the circumstances in your life pushed you to the brink of panic today? Get alone with God. Let Him remind you that nothing you face is bigger or more powerful than He is. And listen to Him whisper over you one more time that He will indeed go with you along the way.

> *Let God's presence be*
> *bigger than your panic.*

❧ Five Minutes in the Word ❧

The heavens declare the glory of God, and the
sky above proclaims his handiwork.

Psalm 19:1

When I look at your heavens, the work of your fingers, the moon
and the stars, which you have set in place, what is man that you
are mindful of him, and the son of man that you care for him?

Psalm 8:3–4

"I pulled you in from all over the world, called you in from every dark
corner of the earth, telling you, 'You're my servant, serving on my
side. I've picked you. I haven't dropped you.' Don't panic. I'm with
you. There's no need to fear for I'm your God. I'll give you strength.
I'll help you. I'll hold you steady, keep a firm grip on you."

Isaiah 41:9–10 THE MESSAGE

You keep him in perfect peace whose mind is stayed
on you, because he trusts in you. Trust in the LORD
forever, for the LORD God is an everlasting rock.

Isaiah 26:3–4

The LORD is my shepherd; I shall not want. He makes me lie down in
green pastures. He leads me beside still waters. He restores my soul.

Psalm 23:1–2

No Longer Shamed

"I f people find out where you've been, no one will ever trust you again!"

I knew what my friend meant. I realized all too clearly that walking away from a well-known Christian ministry to admit myself into a psychiatric hospital was taking a step I never could undo. I was essentially writing my own letter of resignation, not just from who I had been but also from my recent ministry, and perhaps ministry in general. After all, with this act, I was bringing into my life a dark shadow that could have a huge impact on my future.

Mental illness has the curb appeal of festering trash: people give it a wide berth. If I had a brain tumor, reactions would be different. After all, a tumor shows up on an X-ray; it's real. But severe clinical depression can't be X-rayed, so how real can it be?

I'll never forget my first night in the psych ward. I was so afraid. I was alone. I was completely broken. I doubted I would ever feel at peace again as an icy shame enveloped my heart.

Shame means different things to different people. When the psalmist David wrote of shame, he did so with an ancient Near East understanding of that word. To David, *shame* spoke of a life with no hope, a life broken beyond repair. David knew there was only one place to turn—the God of his fathers: "In you, LORD, I have taken refuge; let me never be put to shame; deliver me in your righteousness" (Psalm 31:1 NIV).

David became closer than a brother to me during the first few days of my hospitalization. I would find a quiet spot and pray the psalms out loud. Together he and I moved back and forth from despair to hope, from terror that threatened to swallow us whole to an unshakable trust in the Almighty.

Despite my raw and ragged emotions, I found a peace I'd never known before. It had little to do with where I was and everything to do with *who* I am. When I focused on the beauty of who *I am*—a daughter of the great "I AM"—shame had to bow. Shame was, in fact, dealt its deathblow at the cross of Christ: He who knew no shame became shame for us so that we can be free of it.

So don't allow the enemy to cover you with the trash of your past. In Christ you are loved—and you are free!

> *Shame was dealt a deathblow at the cross of Christ.*

⋙ Five Minutes in the Word ⋘

*Instead of shame and dishonor, you will enjoy a double
share of honor. You will possess a double portion of prosperity
in your land, and everlasting joy will be yours.*

Isaiah 61:7 NLT

*To you they cried and were rescued; in you they
trusted and were not put to shame.*

Psalm 22:5

*[The gospel] is why I am suffering as I am. Yet this is no cause for
shame, because I know whom I have believed, and am convinced
that he is able to guard what I have entrusted to him until that day.*

2 Timothy 1:12 NIV

*In Scripture it says: "See, I lay a stone in Zion, a chosen and precious
cornerstone, and the one who trusts in him will never be put to shame."*

1 Peter 2:6 NIV

In you, O LORD, do I take refuge; let me never be put to shame!

Psalm 71:1

Create in Me a Clean Heart

Y*ou* are the man!" (2 Samuel 12:7).

Nathan's pronouncement echoed throughout the throne room and pierced King David's heart. He had listened to Nathan's story of a wealthy man who had robbed and then deceived a poor man. When David asked who had done this outrageous act, Nathan boldly said, "It's you!"

Blow after blow followed as, speaking on behalf of God, Nathan showed David just how far he had fallen from being the person God intended him to be.

The secret sin David had been hiding as well as the guilt that had been tormenting him were now out in the light. David only had one thing to say: "I have sinned against the LORD" (v. 13).

Nathan immediately assured David that God had forgiven his sin, but still there would be consequences to face. The price of David's transgression was steep: the child he had conceived with Bathsheba, another man's wife, would die.

As painful as it was, Nathan's confrontation of David about his sin was also a great gift because it led David to confession, the first step on the road to healing and restoration. As David himself attested, his guilt had been a terrible burden to bear: "When I kept silent, my bones wasted away through my groaning all day long. For day and night your hand was heavy upon me; my strength was dried up as by the heat of summer" (Psalm 32:3–4). The child born to David and Bathsheba in their sin did die, but when David cast away his mourning garments, he shed his guilt and shame as well.

Bathsheba became David's rightful wife, and God blessed them with a son whom David named Solomon, "the peaceful."

Is there a secret sin weighing heavily on you today? Go to God. Confess it and be free of it. He is waiting for you with the same good news Nathan had for David: your sin has been "put away" (2 Samuel 12:13).

> *Lay down your burden at your Savior's feet,*
> *then lift up your hands in praise.*

ᵦᵒ Five Minutes in the Word ᵒᵦ

*Create in me a clean heart, O God. Renew a loyal spirit
within me. Do not banish me from your presence, and
don't take your Holy Spirit from me. Restore to me the joy
of your salvation, and make me willing to obey you.*

Psalm 51:10–12 NLT

Though we are overwhelmed by our sins, you forgive them all.

Psalm 65:3 NLT

*Praise the LORD, my soul, and forget not all his benefits—who
forgives all your sins and heals all your diseases, who redeems
your life from the pit and crowns you with love and compassion.*

Psalm 103:2–4 NIV

*When people work, their wages are not a gift, but something they
have earned. But people are counted as righteous, not because of
their work, but because of their faith in God who forgives sinners.*

Romans 4:4–5 NLT

*If we claim to be without sin, we deceive ourselves and the truth
is not in us. If we confess our sins, he is faithful and just and will
forgive us our sins and purify us from all unrighteousness.*

1 John 1:8–9 NIV

When the Journey
Is Too Much

"Fatigue makes cowards of us all."

That statement by Green Bay Packers football legend Vince Lombardi is so true. We've all experienced it: the end of the day comes and, with it, the end of our energy and often the end of our courage for whatever the next day may hold. Great heroes of the Bible have experienced it. Even the mighty prophet Elijah.

Our first several encounters with Elijah reveal a fiery man of God, a man unafraid to take on conflict, a man who unhesitatingly took care of the business at hand with, I would venture, a bit of swagger in his step.

When Queen Jezebel found out about all the trouble Elijah had been causing, she threatened his life. I would expect the bold Elijah of Mount Carmel (1 Kings 18) to tell her, "Bring it!"—but that isn't what he did.

Elijah turned and ran. After a day's journey into the wilderness of Judah, Elijah sat down under a broom tree and cried out to God: "It is enough; now, O LORD, take away my life" (1 Kings 19:4).

Wait a minute. What happened to the strong and confident Elijah who stood on Mount Carmel and called down fire from heaven? Keep reading . . .

Immediately after his desperate prayer, Elijah fell asleep under the broom tree (v. 5); he was exhausted.

And what did God do? He didn't lecture Elijah about his calling or tell him to toughen up. No. Instead, God tenderly cared for Elijah. God sent an angel who awakened the prophet to feed him, let him sleep some more, and then fed Elijah again. The food and the rest would enable Elijah to make the journey that lay ahead.

Perhaps a great journey awaits you, or maybe you are traveling a journey that has become too much for you to handle and you're telling God that you've had enough. Take a moment to listen to your body. Do you need a good night's sleep, a power nap, or a solid meal right now?

Your Creator God knows that your physical body has limits. That's why sometimes the most productive thing we can do is simply take a break. It is amazing how a bit of rest can change our perspective, allowing us to experience sweet peace rather than overwhelming anxiety . . . and eventually to recoup our courage!

> *He tenderly and wisely cares for His beloved.*

﹥ᕲ Five Minutes in the Word ᕲ﹤

The apostles returned to Jesus and told him all that they
had done and taught. And he said to them, "Come away
by yourselves to a desolate place and rest a while."

Mark 6:30–31

Truly my soul finds rest in God; my salvation comes from him.

Psalm 62:1 NIV

On the seventh day God had finished his work of creation, so he rested
from all his work. And God blessed the seventh day and declared it holy,
because it was the day when he rested from all his work of creation.

Genesis 2:2–3 NLT

Be still in the presence of the LORD, and wait patiently for him to act.

Psalm 37:7 NLT

"Are you tired? Worn out? Burned out on religion? Come to me. Get away with me and you'll recover your life. I'll show you how to take a real rest. Walk with me and work with me—watch how I do it. Learn the unforced rhythms of grace. I won't lay anything heavy or ill-fitting on you. Keep company with me and you'll learn to live freely and lightly."

Matthew 11:28–30 THE MESSAGE

Making Peace with
Our Limitations

"What time will you get home tomorrow, Mom?" my son asked.

"I'm taking the earliest flight I can, so I'll be home midafternoon," I said.

"Will that give you enough time to get ready for the party?"

"What party?" I asked, a too-familiar feeling of dread rising inside.

The following evening was my son's senior prom. I was speaking in Columbus, Ohio, but since prom pictures weren't until 6:00 p.m. the following day, I knew I'd be home in plenty of time.

"Didn't I tell you about the after-party?" he asked, somewhat sheepishly.

"Nope!" I said.

"I've invited twenty-five friends over after prom," he began. "I'm so sorry. I thought I'd told . . . I mean . . . *asked* you. We won't need much. Just some burgers and pizza. Maybe some brownies."

After I hung up the phone, I buried my head in the hotel pillow and prayed for the return of Christ! *I can't do it all, Lord!*

It's a cold, hard fact: we are finite beings with definite limitations. We have only so much energy and so many hours in the day. If we don't acknowledge that truth and extend ourselves grace for being human, we become shackled with anxiety and feelings of false guilt.

We can make peace with our limitations when we remember that our value rests in *who we are*, not in *what we do.* And hear what the apostle Peter said about who we are: "a chosen people, a royal priesthood, a holy nation, God's special possession . . . the people of God" (1 Peter 2:9–10 NIV).

Sometimes things still have to be done, but they don't have to be perfect. As I prepared for the descending horde, I gave myself permission to do what I could and let the rest go. The house was a little messy but welcoming. The brownies came out of a box, yet they disappeared just as fast as homemade would have. And, more important, everyone had a great time—even me!

> *God loves you for who you are,*
> *not for what you do.*

❧ Five Minutes in the Word ❧

You are the body of Christ, and each one of you is part of it.
1 Corinthians 12:27 NIV

Now that this faith has come, we are no longer under a guardian. So
in Christ Jesus you are all children of God through faith, for all of you
who were baptized into Christ have clothed yourselves with Christ.
Galatians 3:25–27 NIV

As God's chosen people, holy and dearly loved, clothe yourselves
with compassion, kindness, humility, gentleness and patience. Bear
with each other and forgive one another if any of you has a grievance
against someone. Forgive as the Lord forgave you. And over all these
virtues put on love, which binds them all together in perfect unity.
Colossians 3:12–14 NIV

[The Lord] said to me, "My grace is sufficient for you, for my power is made perfect in weakness." Therefore I will boast all the more gladly of my weaknesses, so that the power of Christ may rest upon me.

2 Corinthians 12:9

Let us then with confidence draw near to the throne of grace, that we may receive mercy and find grace to help in time of need.

Hebrews 4:16

"Where Are You?"

It's God's heart-wrenching cry to Adam and Eve: "Where are you?" (Genesis 3:9).

Something had gone terribly wrong. These humans—whom God had made in His image, whom He created to be in relationship with Him, whom He enjoyed meeting with in the cool of the day—were *hiding* from Him.

We can almost hear God's heart breaking as He spoke those words . . . but the rending of God's heart had only begun. Much more sorrow would follow.

From somewhere in the garden, Adam's voice returned God's call. "I heard the sound of you in the garden, and I was afraid" (v. 10).

The following verses reveal the root of the problem: God's children had disobeyed Him and, in doing so, had brought sin and death into the world. Adam and Eve shuddered. Already the darkness of shame had started creeping into their souls and had prompted them to hide from the One who created them and loved them.

Now God had to tell His children what their disobedience would cost them: banishment from Eden; a cursed earth; their own deaths.

But before God pronounced the consequences, He revealed just how He would make things right between Creator and creature. Adam and Eve's disobedience, it turned out, would cost Him more than it cost them. Speaking to the serpent, God said, "I will put enmity between you and the woman, and between your offspring and her offspring; *he shall bruise your head, and you shall bruise his heel*" (v. 15). Right there in Genesis 3, before He sent Adam and Eve out of Eden and posted the angel guard at the gate, God shared His plan to bridge the gap between His children's hearts and His own. God would make a way for the curse of sin—the curse of human separation from Holy God—to be broken. God would send a Redeemer: His Son, Jesus.

Are you hiding from God today? Have you shut off your heart to Him because of mistakes in your past? If so, listen . . . Do you hear the sound of the Father's voice? He is calling you. He created you to be in relationship with Him, and that's what He longs for. Don't be afraid. There's no need to hide. The Messiah has come. Your sins are forgiven. And your Father is waiting.

> **You don't have to hide anymore.**

❧ Five Minutes in the Word ❧

[Jesus] came and preached peace to you who were
far off and peace to those who were near.

Ephesians 2:17

Let us draw near with a true heart in full assurance
of faith, with our hearts sprinkled clean from an evil
conscience and our bodies washed with pure water.

Hebrews 10:22

Most people would not be willing to die for an upright person,
though someone might perhaps be willing to die for a person
who is especially good. But God showed his great love for us
by sending Christ to die for us while we were still sinners.

Romans 5:7–8 NLT

I prayed to the Lord, and he answered me. He freed me from all my fears. Those who look to him for help will be radiant with joy; no shadow of shame will darken their faces.

Psalm 34:4–5 NLT

In [Christ Jesus] and through faith in him we may approach God with freedom and confidence.

Ephesians 3:12 NIV

Waiting ... and at Peace

Café-au-lait skin ... big brown eyes ... a headful of hair going in a million and one directions ... Missy was a darling little girl from Haiti whom one of my dearest friends, Lisa Harper, recently adopted. From the moment she met Missy, Lisa was in love.

But the adoption process was excruciating. Weeks stretched into months and then months into years. Every time it looked as if Missy would finally come home, some new paperwork snafu arose and moved the finish line further into the future. Lisa worried about Missy and *ached* to hold her.

All the while, Missy was growing up—and my friend watched from a distance. There were occasional trips to Port au Prince and photos from time to time.

"I was really bad at waiting," she freely admits. "Waiting truly is one of the hardest things to do on earth."

Yet waiting is part of our reality, and God wants us

to wait peacefully. Key to experiencing peace during the waiting is knowing beyond all doubt that God has heard our prayers.

That knowledge helped Hannah, our Old Testament heroine of the faith. Like my friend, Hannah had been waiting for a child for a very long time, but Hannah's situation was made even more painful by her husband's second wife, Peninnah. Having been blessed with several children, Peninnah loved to torment Hannah about the fact that her womb remained empty. In 1 Samuel 1, we read that Peninnah had been so horrible to Hannah each time they were at Shiloh for the annual feast that Hannah had been "reduced to tears and would not even eat" (v. 7 NLT). It had happened year after year.

Hannah had taken all she could take. She fled to the house of the Lord and poured out to Him her anguished heart. After she finished praying, Hannah finally got an answer that brought peace to her soul. The priest Eli said, "Go in peace, and may the God of Israel grant you what you have asked of him" (v. 17 NIV).

The next verse tells us that she returned to her family but was "no longer downcast."

Maybe you are waiting today.

Waiting for a child . . .

Or for provision . . .

Or for an answer . . .

Let Hannah lead the way. Pour out your soul to God and be confident that He hears you. May you rest in the peace of that promise while you wait.

> **God is with you in the meantime.**

⟡ Five Minutes in the Word ⟡

In my alarm I said, "I am cut off from your sight!" Yet you heard my cry for mercy when I called to you for help. Love the LORD, all his faithful people! The LORD preserves those who are true to him, but the proud he pays back in full. Be strong and take heart, all you who hope in the LORD.
Psalm 31:22–24 NIV

I remain confident of this: I will see the goodness of the LORD in the land of the living. Wait for the LORD; be strong and take heart and wait for the LORD.
Psalm 27:13–14 NIV

This is what the Sovereign LORD, the Holy One of Israel,
says: "Only in returning to me and resting in me will you be
saved. In quietness and confidence is your strength."

Isaiah 30:15 NLT

[The LORD] gives power to the faint, and to him who has no might
he increases strength. Even youths shall faint and be weary, and
young men shall fall exhausted; but they who wait for the LORD shall
renew their strength; they shall mount up with wings like eagles;
they shall run and not be weary; they shall walk and not faint.

Isaiah 40:29–31

May integrity and uprightness preserve me, for I wait for you.

Psalm 25:21

Our Shelter and Our Refuge

How did he survive?

What did he do to stay sane?

What enabled him to hold on to hope?

If we had lived in Great Britain around AD 430, we might have asked these questions of a young man named Patricius. At the age of sixteen, this well-educated Roman citizen and cherished son was brutally snatched from his home and taken to Ireland as a slave.

Patricius spent six years hungry, cold, and in nearly complete isolation. What enabled him to endure the abuse, neglect, and trauma? How could this brutalized young person ultimately become an influential man of God?

On the desolate hills of Ireland, with the sheep he tended as his only companions, young Patricius prayed. Moment by moment, every hour of the day and night, he turned his heart toward God in prayer. Patricius clung to the only One who could hold him together in such difficult circumstances.

And along the way something beautiful happened: Patricius was changed. Author Thomas Cahill put it this way: "Patricius endured six years of this woeful isolation, and by the end of it he had grown from a careless boy to something he would surely never otherwise have become—a holy man, indeed a visionary for whom there was no longer any rigid separation between this world and the next."[2]

Ultimately, God granted Patricius his freedom, and he returned home to Great Britain. But Patricius didn't live the rest of his days in well-deserved comfort. How could he, when the cries of the unsaved Irish haunted him?

He returned to Ireland, the land of his oppression, and shared with the people the light of God's love. We know him today as Saint Patrick.

In a world of trouble (John 16:33), there will be casualties—and we believers in Christ are not guaranteed immunity from the carnage. What we are promised is that out of the worst circumstances this world can hurl at us, we who are God's children are never alone. In fact, in times of suffering . . . He is our Shelter!

Like Patricius, we can be absolutely confident that as we stay close to God and allow Him to do His good work in us, He will bring beautiful things out of the trials we face.

> *God is a shelter for His children and a*
> *Redeemer who brings beauty out of ashes.*

⚬⚭ Five Minutes in the Word ⚮⚬

Guard me as you would guard your own eyes.
Hide me in the shadow of your wings.

Psalm 17:8 NLT

In the day of trouble [the LORD] will keep me safe in his dwelling; he will
hide me in the shelter of his sacred tent and set me high upon a rock.

Psalm 27:5 NIV

How great is the goodness you have stored up for those who fear you. You lavish
it on those who come to you for protection, blessing them before the watching
world. You hide them in the shelter of your presence, safe from those who conspire
against them. You shelter them in your presence, far from accusing tongues.

Psalm 31:19–20 NLT

Be merciful to me, O God, be merciful to me, for in you
my soul takes refuge; in the shadow of your wings I will
take refuge, till the storms of destruction pass by.

Psalm 57:1

"Neither Do I Condemn You"

N ow in the Law Moses commanded us to stone such women. So what do you say?" (John 8:5).

The woman caught in the act of adultery hung her head in shame. The crowd around Jesus was quiet, awaiting His response to the hostile scribes and Pharisees.

It was a trap, and Jesus knew it. If He sided with the woman, He stood in opposition to God's law. If He sided with the law, He stood against the woman in her hour of greatest need. Would Jesus choose judgment or mercy? Would He choose to uphold the law, or would He risk His own reputation and possibly His own safety for the sake of the obviously guilty woman? The Pharisees were sure they had cornered Jesus this time. The woman meant nothing to them at all—she was merely the bait in their trap. But Jesus wanted to help her.

You can read this remarkable story in its entirety in John 8:1–11, but let me share some highlights. Jesus, of course, chose mercy over judgment, and He did it in a way that had her accusers quietly retreating from the temple courts. Once the woman was safely delivered from them, He got about the business of healing her sin-wounded heart:

> Jesus stood up and said to her, "Woman, where are they? Has no one condemned you?"
>
> She said, "No one, Lord,"
>
> And Jesus said, "Neither do I condemn you; go, and from now on sin no more." (vv. 10–11)

Perhaps you, like the woman in this story, feel the weight of your accusers' judgment or the sting of their condemning glances. Maybe your failings have been talked about around town for much too long. If so, remember this: Condemnation is always horizontal. It is something we fallen children of Adam and Eve do to one another.

So choose vertical instead of horizontal. Grace begins at the cross of Christ. Look up to the One who loved you enough to die for the sins others mock. And if you are struggling with shame today, know that Jesus has for you the same compassionate words He spoke to the woman caught in adultery: "Neither do I condemn you. Go and sin no more."

Let Jesus' words bring peace to your weary heart.

> *Grace meets us in the dust, but*
> *He never leaves us there.*

✥ Five Minutes in the Word ✥

Since we have been justified by faith, we have peace
with God through our Lord Jesus Christ.

Romans 5:1

There is therefore now no condemnation for
those who are in Christ Jesus.

Romans 8:1

"God did not send his Son into the world to condemn the world,
but in order that the world might be saved through him."

John 3:17

The LORD redeems the life of his servants; none of those
who take refuge in him will be condemned.

Psalm 34:22

By this we shall know that we are of the truth and reassure
our heart before him; for whenever our heart condemns us,
God is greater than our heart, and he knows everything.

1 John 3:19–20

Thelma and Louise

I remember the first time we met. She was in my book-signing line, and she was in a wheelchair. I tried to help her move her chair a little so she would be at a better angle for the photograph, but I touched the wrong button and sent her flying backward into the crowd. Thankfully neither she nor the crowd held it against me!

After that she and I became friends. Her name is Erin, and she was born with spastic cerebral palsy quadriplegia. At fourteen, scoliosis was added to her diagnosis. Since then depression has moved in as well.

Every year when I'm speaking at an event in the arena closest to her city, she comes. I know it's not easy for her, but she finds a way. It was at a smaller event in the spring of 2015 that took it to a whole new level!

Erin told me that she and her best friend, Jen, also in a wheelchair, would be there. Knowing they would be traveling quite a distance from home, I asked Erin if they were staying in a hotel for the night. She said they were. I made sure that the event planners reserved a table for them with enough room for their chairs. At the end of the evening, I joined Erin and Jen for coffee, and we talked and laughed until it was time to call it a night. As my host was pulling up her car, I asked my friend if she would text me when they got to their hotel so I'd know they'd made it safely. She promised she would.

Eleven o'clock came and went . . . then midnight . . . and I began to get really worried. Finally, the text came in, the truth was out—and I almost swallowed my tonsils.

Erin and Jen were never in a vehicle that night. They had headed off down the road in their chairs, and when they ran out of power, they had to pull into a bar to recharge!

As I pictured this Thelma and Louise of the evangelical world plugged in beside the bikers and pool tables, I marveled again at what it costs some people to follow Christ. Erin is honest with me. She shares her frustrations and fears just as she shares her victories and moments of rest, and she usually closes her texts with #BelievingGod.

Years ago my good friend Joni Erickson Tada, also a quadriplegic, told me that she thought the faith journey was harder for me than for her. I asked why.

"Because I can't even for a moment forget my need for Christ; you can."

Powerful, hard-won words.

So today I encourage you to sit down . . . to be still . . . to cast your cares upon Him and remember that He is everything we need to know if we want to know peace.

> *When you are running on empty, stop and intentionally plug into Christ.*

❧ Five Minutes in the Word ❧

"Be still, and know that I am God."

Psalm 46:10

Thus said the Lord GOD, the Holy One of Israel, "In returning and rest you shall be saved; in quietness and in trust shall be your strength."

Isaiah 30:15

The result of righteousness will be peace; the effect of righteousness will be quiet confidence forever.

Isaiah 32:17 HCSB

The Lord is at hand; do not be anxious about anything, but in everything by prayer and supplication with thanksgiving let your requests be made known to God. And the peace of God, which surpasses all understanding, will guard your hearts and your minds in Christ Jesus.

Philippians 4:5–7

Help My Unbelief!

To say that the scene was tense would be an understatement.

Jesus' disciples were arguing with the teachers of the law, and a crowd had gathered to watch. In the center of the scene stood a demon-possessed boy and his father, a man broken by discouragement and hopelessness.

And maybe you understand . . . much better than you wish. You too have been on a most difficult journey. Yes, you started out strong, but as the days grew into weary weeks and then months, as your most fervent prayers seemed to bounce right back to you from the ceiling above, your faith began to wear thin. Now, broken by discouragement, you stand in the middle of the chaos desperate for deliverance but too tired to scrounge up even a teaspoonful of hope.

When Jesus approached the crowd, He spoke to the exhausted father:

"How long has this been happening to him?"

And [the father] said, "From childhood. And it has often cast him into fire and into water, to destroy him. But if you can do anything, have compassion on us and help us."

And Jesus said to him, "'If you can'! All things are possible for the one who believes."

Immediately the father of the child cried out and said, "I believe; help my unbelief!" (Mark 9:21–24)

And that is what Jesus did. He met the father right where he was on the continuum between belief and unbelief, and Jesus set his son free.

So if you are weary in your faith today, this is what I want you to remember about this story: admittedly, the father's faith wasn't spectacular, but Jesus still acted. Jesus didn't need anyone to have perfect faith; He healed the boy anyway.

Jesus doesn't need us to have perfect faith either. Simply offer God whatever faith you have today, no matter how small, frayed, battered, or worn.

Jesus doesn't condemn you or me for a faith that is weaker than we wish it were. He loves you, and He will act.

> *We don't need perfect faith when
> we have a perfect Savior.*

⤳ Five Minutes in the Word ⤳

*"Truly I tell you, if you have faith as small as a mustard
seed, you can say to this mountain, 'Move from here to there,'
and it will move. Nothing will be impossible for you."*
Matthew 17:20 NIV

Your steadfast love is before my eyes, and I walk in your faithfulness.
Psalm 26:3

*Be truly glad. There is wonderful joy ahead, even though you
must endure many trials for a little while. These trials will
show that your faith is genuine. It is being tested as fire tests
and purifies gold—though your faith is far more precious than
mere gold. So when your faith remains strong through many
trials, it will bring you much praise and glory and honor on
the day when Jesus Christ is revealed to the whole world.*
1 Peter 1:6–7 NLT

May the God of peace himself sanctify you completely, and may your whole spirit and soul and body be kept blameless at the coming of our Lord Jesus Christ. He who calls you is faithful; he will surely do it.

1 Thessalonians 5:23–24

Now all glory to God, who is able to keep you from falling away and will bring you with great joy into his glorious presence without a single fault.

Jude v. 24 NLT

Come as You Are

One of the challenges of flying is that sometimes I arrive in one city and my luggage arrives in another. It was easier before the devastating events of 9/11 to keep everything together, especially since we could carry larger quantities of liquids in our carry-ons. I try to remember to buy small cans of hair spray and squeeze my shampoo and conditioner into the little regulation-size plastic bottles sold everywhere, but as I'm often running at the last minute, I inevitably have to check one bag. The lesson I learned in the spring of 2014, however, taught me *always* to keep something to wear on the platform in my carry-on.

I was speaking at a conference for a very conservative denomination. The airport closest to this small town in Missouri was in St. Louis. After waiting at baggage claim for thirty minutes, I realized that my bag had no love for St. Louis and had rerouted itself. It was late and the mall was closed. The sweet lady who picked me up for the three-hour drive told me not to worry—in the small town where we were headed was a certain twenty-four-hour, large chain store. I wasn't so sure that this store even sold clothes!

We headed to the makeup section first, and I quickly picked out two shades of foundation. Having used the stab-in-the-dark color-matching method, I was fully aware I might end up looking like an albino rabbit or a woman from West Africa. We moved to the clothes section, which, we were told, had a very low inventory because of a recent large event in town. I found one dress that . . . fit me. Had I been four inches taller, it would have fit better, but the upside was, I'd be in an acceptable outfit and sweep the platform at the same time!

When I looked at myself in the mirror that next morning, I didn't know whether to laugh or cry. I'd mixed the two shades of foundation, but I was still a peculiar color. As for my outfit, I looked like a reject from *Little House on the Prairie*!

Well, Lord! What do You think? I asked.

And what did I hear in my spirit?

"Beautiful!"

No, God's not color-blind or fashion challenged. He just sees the real you no matter what the mirror says.

We live in a world where we are judged every day on what will never last. Peace comes from being seen and loved just as we are.

> *God looks at you today and calls you beautiful because He sees the lovely you who will never fade.*

⚬ Five Minutes in the Word ⚬

"The LORD bless you and keep you; the LORD make his face shine on you and be gracious to you; the LORD turn his face toward you and give you peace."

Numbers 6:23–26 NIV

I keep my eyes always on the LORD. With him at my right hand, I will not be shaken. Therefore my heart is glad and my tongue rejoices; my body also will rest secure.

Psalm 16:8–9 NIV

To all who did receive [Jesus], who believed in his name, he gave the right to become children of God.

John 1:12

"Why do you worry about clothes? See how the flowers of the field grow. They do not labor or spin. Yet I tell you that not even Solomon in all his splendor was dressed like one of these."

Matthew 6:28–29 NIV

Let your adorning be the hidden person of the heart with the imperishable beauty of a gentle and quiet spirit, which in God's sight is very precious.

1 Peter 3:4

Good News for All . . .
Means You Too

Spring had sprung, and prom season was blooming. Seventeen-year-old high school quarterback Ben Moser knew who he'd be going with. Back in fourth grade, he had made a promise to his friend Mary: when the time came to choose his prom date, he would ask her.

Fourth-grade Ben was simply doing what he had been doing faithfully since second grade. He was making sure Mary, who has Down syndrome, was included.

Why do stories like this one capture our hearts and burn up the Internet like wildfire? Because they offer a resounding "Yes!" to the question each of us has from time to time: *Is it possible for me to be accepted and loved just as I am? Am I enough?*

If the shepherds in Luke 2 had ever asked themselves those questions, they got an unforgettable answer. Let me set the scene.

At the time of the Savior's birth, shepherds were regarded as untrustworthy. They were considered to be on the lower rungs of society. How amazing that God chose these who were considered "less than" to hear the angel announce the Savior's birth! Listen to this beautiful greeting: "Fear not, for behold, I bring you good news of great joy that will be *for all the people.* For unto you is born this day in the city of David a Savior, who is Christ the Lord" (vv. 10–11).

All the people . . .

The shepherds might have been rejected by society, by fellow human beings, but not by God. The eternal and almighty One wanted them to know that He loved them and accepted them just as they were.

And that, my friend, was very good news for the shepherds, and it is very good news for us.

Are you struggling to know that you are accepted and loved just as you are, that you are enough? There is no need to fear. God loves you and accepts you no matter your failings, no matter your past. Allow your heart to rest in His great love for you.

> *The people who walked in the darkness of*
> *doubt have seen the great light of God's love.*

⟿ Five Minutes in the Word ⟾

You are a chosen race, a royal priesthood, a holy nation, a people
for his own possession, that you may proclaim the excellencies of
him who called you out of darkness into his marvelous light.

1 Peter 2:9

The Spirit of the Sovereign LORD is upon me, for the LORD has anointed me to
bring good news to the poor. He has sent me to comfort the brokenhearted
and to proclaim that captives will be released and prisoners will be freed.

Isaiah 61:1 NLT

For a child will be born for us, a son will be given to us, and the
government will be on His shoulders. He will be named Wonderful
Counselor, Mighty God, Eternal Father, Prince of Peace.

Isaiah 9:6 HCSB

Who dares accuse us whom God has chosen for his own? No one—
for God himself has given us right standing with himself.

Romans 8:33 NLT

Meals That Matter

Five-year-old Josiah didn't understand what he was seeing as he sat with his mom at their local Waffle House. A man sat alone in a booth nearby. He was visibly dirty. His clothes were ragged and his posture weary. Although he lingered, no one came to take his order.

"Why does the man look that way?" Josiah wanted to know.

His mother replied that the man was homeless.

"What does *homeless* mean?"

"Well, he doesn't have a house to live in."

Josiah—like the Old Testament king of Judah—was born to be a man of righteous action. Young Josiah wanted his mom to buy the man a meal—and he wouldn't take no for an answer. When she agreed, he sprang from his chair with a menu in hand and approached the stranger.

"You can't order without a menu," he said.

Soon the hamburger with extra bacon arrived, but

as the hungry man leaned in for a bite, Josiah stopped him. They needed to thank God for the food first!

As the man bowed his head, tears ran down his cheeks. The rest of the customers watched in holy silence as Josiah's sweet, clear voice filled the place.

"Thank You for our blessings," he sang. "Thank You for our blessings. Amen. Amen."[3]

What a poignant picture of love in action Josiah offered the onlookers in that sacred moment.

At another meal two thousand years ago, another picture of love in action unfolded. As Jesus broke the bread and passed the wine during the last Passover meal He would share with His disciples, He said, "Do this in remembrance of me" (Luke 22:19).

The breaking of the bread would forevermore symbolize the breaking of His body as He took on the punishment for our sins. The pouring of the wine would remind us of His blood shed for our sins.

Jesus thanked the Father for these elements before sharing them with His closest followers. Jesus offered those thanks despite the gathering storm of the cross. And knowing that His death on the cross would bridge the great divide between God and man that was cleft by sin—knowing that the cross would enable His disciples to become His friends—Jesus commanded them, "Do this and remember!"

Like Josiah's new friend in the Waffle House, we are the broken—we are the hungry, the filthy, the lonely—until we take the bread and the wine. We pause to remember the One who gave His life to make us, the homeless, His friends.

What amazing love.

> *Jesus' love in action means wholeness for the broken—and all of us are broken by sin.*

ᴥᴥ Five Minutes in the Word ᴥᴥ

"No longer do I call you servants, for the servant does not know
what his master is doing; but I have called you friends, for all
that I have heard from my Father I have made known to you."

John 15:15

He was pierced for our transgressions, he was crushed
for our iniquities; the punishment that brought us peace
was on him, and by his wounds we are healed.

Isaiah 53:5 NIV

Jesus said, "Father, forgive them, for they
don't know what they are doing."

Luke 23:34 NLT

"Come now, let us reason together, says the LORD: though your
sins are like scarlet, they shall be as white as snow; though
they are red like crimson, they shall become like wool."

Isaiah 1:18

[Jesus] took some bread and gave thanks to God for it. Then he
broke it in pieces and gave it to the disciples, saying, "This is
my body, which is given for you. Do this to remember me." After
supper he took another cup of wine and said, "This cup is the new
covenant between God and his people—an agreement confirmed
with my blood, which is poured out as a sacrifice for you."

Luke 22:19–20 NLT

Sharing the Peace of Christ

Since our son, Christian, headed off to his first year of college, I've been feeling a little nostalgic and thinking back on some of my favorite memories from his growing-up years. One of them involved four turkeys and ten pairs of sunglasses!

Christian is a December baby and was about to turn five that year. He and Barry were with me on the road as I was touring with a children's Christmas musical. Christian loved the tour bus. He would crawl into his bunk, put his favorite movie into the DVD player, and be rocked to sleep as we rolled on to the next city.

We had a show on Wednesday, November 21, and one on Friday, November 23, but Thanksgiving Day was free. After asking the other performers what they were doing to celebrate, I realized that none of them would be able to travel home for Thanksgiving and be back in time for Friday's show. I came up with a plan.

Our house was nearby, and so with a little help from the bus driver and a few sleeping bags borrowed from neighbors, we all headed that way after Wednesday's show. One of my best friends went shopping for me and traded in my one little turkey for four beauties. We got home late that night, and everyone bunked down wherever they could while I started cooking. I wanted this to be a memorable Thanksgiving for everyone.

When the feast was finally ready the next day, we took our seats in the sunroom, which had been converted to a makeshift dining room. Only one problem: everyone facing the window was blinded by the late autumn sun. Christian said, "I've got this, Mom!" He flew up to his room and came back with ten pairs of silly sunglasses we were saving for his birthday party.

It was quite a sight: Twenty people gathered round four stuffed birds with ten of us wearing shades! But the memory I treasure most was what everyone shared that day. One by one we gave thanks to God for the blessings of that year and the gift of friends. Everyone signed a guest book as they left, and later Christian asked if he could see what they had written. Each one of them had shared a Scripture verse that had encouraged and strengthened them. For many it was a life verse, a star to sail their ship by. Christian brought his Bible down, and we marked every single verse. On that Thanksgiving, we were beyond grateful.

> **When we open our hearts and our homes,
> we share the peace of Christ.**

✤ Five Minutes in the Word ✤

*Do not neglect to show hospitality to strangers, for
thereby some have entertained angels unawares.*

Hebrews 13:2

*"'I was hungry and you gave me food, I was thirsty and you gave
me drink, I was a stranger and you welcomed me, I was naked and
you clothed me, I was sick and you visited me, I was in prison and
you came to me.' Then the righteous will answer him, saying, 'Lord,
when did we see you hungry and feed you, or thirsty and give you
drink? And when did we see you a stranger and welcome you, or
naked and clothe you? And when did we see you sick or in prison
and visit you?' And the King will answer them, 'Truly, I say to you, as
you did it to one of the least of these my brothers, you did it to me.'"*

Matthew 25:35–40

Love never fails.

1 Corinthians 13:8 NIV

Jesus replied: "'Love the Lord your God with all your heart and with all your soul and with all your mind.' This is the first and greatest commandment. And the second is like it: 'Love your neighbor as yourself.'"

Matthew 22:37–39 NIV

Level Ground

One day a friend of mine walked in on her teenage son watching a particularly cutthroat reality TV show.

"Why do you think we like to watch shows like that?" she asked him.

"I don't know," he responded. "I guess because they're funny."

"I don't think that's why we like them," she said, and left it at that.

Later, he went to find her. "So what is the reason, Mom? Why do you think we like to watch reality TV?"

"I think it's because watching someone behave horribly allows us to feel better about ourselves. You know, an 'At least I'm not like that!' sort of thing."

It has often been said that the ground is level at the foot of the cross: every human being is a sinner in need of forgiveness and salvation; none of us sinners is better than any of our fellow sinners. That statement is very true . . . and very difficult to remember.

Rather than looking at our own sin, we find it much easier—and even comforting—to squint at the person beside us and imagine that the ground slopes a bit, with us standing on the higher ground. How tempting it is to size up our neighbor's failings that, at least in our estimation, are far worse than ours!

But consider Jesus' perspective on sin: "You have heard that it was said to those of old, 'You shall not murder; and whoever murders will be liable to judgment.' But I say to you that everyone who is angry with his brother will be liable to judgment" (Matthew 5:21–22).

Yes, you read that right. Jesus equated unjust anger at our neighbor with murder! And that's because Jesus knows that righteousness isn't about keeping a set of rules; righteousness—and therefore sin—is a matter of the heart.

The good news is that Jesus paid the price for our sins . . . and for the sins of all people throughout all time. All of us have sinned.

How are you seeing your fellow sinners today? Do you see people whose bad choices make you feel just a little bit superior? Or do you see someone dearly loved by God who needs His grace just as much as you so desperately do? Even in your attitude and silent thoughts, extend to others the grace you yourself have received.

After all, the ground truly *is* level before the cross of Christ.

> *How could we ever kneel at the cross of*
> *Christ and point the finger at another sinner?*

⟶ Five Minutes in the Word ⟵

We have all become like one who is unclean, and all
our righteous deeds are like a polluted garment.

Isaiah 64:6

If possible, so far as it depends on you, live peaceably with all.

Romans 12:18

We are made right with God by placing our faith in Jesus Christ.
And this is true for everyone who believes, no matter who we are. For
everyone has sinned; we all fall short of God's glorious standard.

Romans 3:22–23 NLT

"A new commandment I give to you, that you love one another:
just as I have loved you, you also are to love one another."

John 13:34

It is by grace you have been saved, through faith—and this is not from
yourselves, it is the gift of God—not by works, so that no one can boast.

Ephesians 2:8–9 NIV

Perfect Peace

Poor Nicholas Herman didn't have much going for him. Even after he dedicated his life to Christ and became a monk, he found himself on the periphery of the monastic community. (That must have been a hard pill to swallow. You've dedicated your whole life to serve God and entered the monastery only to find out that you're at the bottom of the monk totem pole!) His job working in the kitchen was simple enough, but there were reports that he was constantly breaking things and, as a result, finding himself the target of the other brothers' ridicule.

A monk's life was not an easy one to begin with, but add to that a menial job, daily failure, and personal isolation from his community. It would be easy to conclude that Nicholas was utterly miserable.

Strangely enough, though, Nicholas—who took the name Brother Lawrence when he became a monk—lived a life of deep contentment and peace. As a matter of fact, he was so obviously joyful and at peace that people began asking him the reason for his joy and the basis of his peace.

Brother Lawrence told them the answer was simple but a matter of tremendous discipline. He told them that he "practiced the presence of God" moment by moment: he never allowed his heart to wander from the heart of his beloved Savior. According to Brother Lawrence, "we should feed and nourish our souls with high notions of God."[4] Even if he peeled potatoes, he did it for the glory of God.

The Bible provides some pretty good evidence that Brother Lawrence was onto something. Listen to Isaiah 26:3, for instance: "You will keep him in perfect peace whose mind is stayed on you, because he trusts in you."

The book of Isaiah was written to a people who were in serious trouble. The northern kingdom of Israel had been carried into a captivity from which they would never return. The southern kingdom of Judah was facing the storm of her own approaching judgment. But here and there in Isaiah, among dire warnings of the dark days to come, God graciously wove a bright thread of the redemptive peace found in Him alone.

Maybe you, like Brother Lawrence, have looked around and felt like nothing was working for you.

Or perhaps, like Israel, you received news that meant the road ahead would be long, difficult, and dark.

Keep your heart and mind on Jesus. Like Brother Lawrence, you can learn to discipline a wandering mind and to keep refocusing your thoughts on Christ.

> *When we fix our gaze on Christ,*
> *He fills our hearts with peace.*

⁓ Five Minutes in the Word ⁓

For a day in your courts is better than a thousand
elsewhere. I would rather be a doorkeeper in the house
of my God than dwell in the tents of wickedness.

Psalm 84:10

He who dwells in the shelter of the Most High will abide
in the shadow of the Almighty. I will say to the Lord, "My
refuge and my fortress, my God, in whom I trust."

Psalm 91:1–2

Let us run with endurance the race God has set before us.
We do this by keeping our eyes on Jesus, the champion who
initiates and perfects our faith. Because of the joy awaiting
him, he endured the cross, disregarding its shame. Now he
is seated in the place of honor beside God's throne.

Hebrews 12:1–2 NLT

Set your minds on things that are above,
not on things that are on earth.

Colossians 3:2

Great peace have those who love your law,
and nothing can make them stumble.

Psalm 119:165 NIV

What Is Forgiveness?

It was a conversation I wasn't supposed to hear.

Wanting another cup of coffee, I'd asked two of my coworkers if they needed a refill. They said yes. Halfway to the break room I realized I hadn't asked if they took sugar and cream, so I backtracked just in time to hear, "I've never liked her. She's just Little Miss Perfect!"

"Keep your voice down! She'll be back in a minute!" the other replied, laughing.

"You know how her cash register was short last night?" the first girl asked. "I did that, and I'm going to get her fired."

I stood for a moment, face flushed, heart in my stomach. I was eighteen years old, working in a department store for the summer, and I didn't know what to do. *Should I confront her? Should I report her? Should I just quit?*

I decided to confront her—but not until I had forgiven her. And forgiving her gave me the courage to speak the truth.

It's easy, though, to get confused about forgiveness, about what it *is* and what it *is not*.

Forgiveness is not being a doormat and abandoning all boundaries so that the other person can walk all over us.

Forgiveness also doesn't mean we necessarily have to stay in relationship with the other person. When His disciples were going out to do ministry, Jesus told them that if they encountered someone who would not listen to them or did not welcome them, they should shake the dust off their feet and leave (Matthew 10:14).

What, then, is forgiveness?

Forgiveness is a practice we Christians are called to incorporate into our daily lives. In the Lord's Prayer, Jesus clearly connected our willingness to forgive others with the forgiveness we receive from God (Luke 11:4).

Forgiveness is also trusting God with the hurt we have experienced. Romans 12:19 tells us, "Beloved, never avenge yourselves, but leave it to the wrath of God, for it is written, 'Vengeance is mine, I will repay, says the Lord.'"

True freedom and peace come when we realize that we may not be able to trust the person who hurt us, but we can trust our good and loving God with our hurt. We can also release to God the person who hurt us. And *that* is forgiveness.

> *Forgiveness is God's gift to us: it enables*
> *us to live in a world that's not fair.*

⌒ Five Minutes in the Word ⌒

"I, the LORD, love justice; I hate robbery and wrongdoing.
In my faithfulness I will reward my people and
make an everlasting covenant with them."

Isaiah 61:8 NIV

"If you forgive those who sin against you, your heavenly
Father will forgive you. But if you refuse to forgive
others, your Father will not forgive your sins."

Matthew 6:14–15 NLT

"God blesses those who work for peace, for they will be called the
children of God. God blesses those who are persecuted for doing
right, for the Kingdom of Heaven is theirs. God blesses you when
people mock you and persecute you and lie about you and say all sorts
of evil things against you because you are my followers. Be happy
about it! Be very glad! For a great reward awaits you in heaven."

Matthew 5:9–12 NLT

Be completely humble and gentle; be patient, bearing with one another in love. Make every effort to keep the unity of the Spirit through the bond of peace.

Ephesians 4:2–3 NIV

Now the Lord is the Spirit, and where the Spirit of the Lord is, there is freedom.

2 Corinthians 3:17 NIV

Cradled in the Freefall

F or as long as I live, I will not let this suffering be normal," Kayla Jean Mueller vowed.

The quiet young woman packed her bags and did what she had done before as an aid worker in India, Israel, and Palestine. Kayla Jean had again looked around to see where refugees were fleeing terror and suffering. She saw where she would find hungry and sick children, and she ran straight toward it.

This time she headed to Syria. And there she comforted those who were suffering . . . until the day she encountered a thick darkness of her own.

Kayla Jean's suffering began when masked men carrying guns took her captive. Her suffering ended with her tragic death. You may have heard of her death on the national news, but what wasn't reported was her passionate relationship with Christ.

Soon after her death, Kayla Jean's parents released

a letter she had written to them while she was being held captive. Intended to comfort her family, what she wrote is a great testimony of her Christian faith. Listen for how Kayla Jean teaches us how to be at peace in the most horrific of circumstances: "I have surrendered myself to our Creator because literally, there was no one else. . . . By God and by your prayers, I have felt tenderly cradled in freefall."[5]

Surrender? Oh, how we wish there were some other way, don't we? We are Adam's sons and Eve's daughters, and we balk at the idea of surrendering. To us who are children of the fall, surrender feels like death . . . but it isn't. Surrender is actually the gateway to life!

I wonder how often, when He watches my struggle to surrender, Jesus cries out with words similar to what He said to Israel: "O Jerusalem, Jerusalem. . . . How often would I have gathered your children together as a hen gathers her brood under her wings, and you were not willing!" (Matthew 23:37).

Notice the tenderness of that imagery. Jesus longs to draw us close to His heart, to keep us safely under His wings, just like a mother hen gathers her chicks. The Father's heart toward you is loving, good, and kind. Don't resist Him, not for one more day. Surrender yourself to Him and let Him draw you close. He longs to tenderly cradle us in freefall, just as He did Kayla Jean.

> **When you find yourself falling,**
> **remember you are held.**

⚬ Five Minutes in the Word ⚬

If I say, "Surely the darkness shall cover me, and the light
about me be night," even the darkness is not dark to you; the
night is bright as the day, for darkness is as light with you.

Psalm 139:11–12

I can never escape from your Spirit! I can never get away
from your presence! If I go up to heaven, you are there; if I
go down to the grave, you are there. If I ride the wings of the
morning, if I dwell by the farthest oceans, even there your
hand will guide me, and your strength will support me.

Psalm 139:7–10 NLT

Have I not commanded you? Be strong and courageous! Do not tremble
or be dismayed, for the LORD your God is with you wherever you go.

Joshua 1:9 NASB

"You are my servant, I have chosen you and not cast you off; fear not, for I am with you; be not dismayed, for I am your God. I will strengthen you, I will help you, I will uphold you with my righteous right hand."

Isaiah 41:9–10

"I am the light of the world. Whoever follows me will not walk in darkness, but will have the light of life."

John 8:12

Entrusted with a Test

The desperate woman shouted to get the Savior's attention: "Have mercy on me, O Lord, Son of David; my daughter is severely oppressed by a demon" (Matthew 15:22).

This Canaanite woman begging for Jesus' help was everything traditional Jewish culture considered "less than," but Jesus saw her remarkable faith. And He decided to entrust her with a difficult test: He would temporarily refuse her plea to help her daughter. Would her faith be strong enough to enable her to pass the test?

The mother's pitiful cry lingered in the air, and Jesus ignored her.

So she fell to her knees at His feet. "Help me," she pleaded (v. 25).

Jesus' response sounds harsh: "It is not right to take the children's bread and throw it to the dogs" (v. 26).

The crowd must have gasped, but the woman's faith held strong: "Yes, Lord, yet even the dogs eat the crumbs that fall from their master's table" (v. 27). She passed the test!

At that point Jesus spoke words of commendation as well as words she had longed to hear: "O woman, great is your faith! Be it done for you as you desire" (v. 28).

She finally received what she had longed for. She had undoubtedly asked hard questions until this moment—and maybe they are questions you've asked: *What is God doing? Why hasn't He delivered us, provided for us, cured us? Why is His heart so callous and cold?*

But a callous, cold God—an indifferent, heartless God—simply isn't possible. Such a God would totally contradict everything else the love story of Scripture tells us about our Creator and Redeemer. Our God hears the cry of the afflicted (Psalm 10:17), and He draws near to the brokenhearted (Psalm 34:18).

When we don't understand what is happening, let us consider that unfolding before us is a bigger, more complex plan than we are able to see.

Consider, too, that as He did in His interaction with the Canaanite woman, Jesus may be honoring us with a difficult test. When by His grace we pass, we will bring great glory to His name.

When times are desperate, may we, like the Canaanite woman, cling to what we know to be true of Jesus: He is good. He is kind. He is compassionate.

And may these truths bring peace to our souls as we wait for deliverance to come.

> *Trust in the heart of God even when you cannot see the work His hands are doing.*

﹋ Five Minutes in the Word ﹌

Though you have not seen him, you love him; and even though
you do not see him now, you believe in him and are filled
with an inexpressible and glorious joy, for you are receiving
the end result of your faith, the salvation of your souls.

1 Peter 1:8–9 NIV

Be on your guard; stand firm in the faith; be
courageous, be strong. Do everything in love.

1 Corinthians 16:13–14 NIV

Faith is confidence in what we hope for and
assurance about what we do not see.

Hebrews 11:1 NIV

Jesus told [Thomas], "Because you have seen me, you have believed;
blessed are those who have not seen and yet have believed."

John 20:29 NIV

Our earthly fathers disciplined us for a few years, doing the best they knew how. But God's discipline is always good for us, so that we might share in his holiness. No discipline is enjoyable while it is happening—it's painful! But afterward there will be a peaceful harvest of right living for those who are trained in this way.

Hebrews 12:10–11 NLT

Looking Back at God's Faithfulness

When my son, Christian, was ten years old, he gave me a Promise Box. He made it himself, and it's one of the sweetest gifts he's ever given me. The edges are a little rough, and a few of the mirrored tiles he glued on have fallen off, but I treasure it.

When he presented it to me, he said, "It's to keep all the promises God gives you, Mom."

I lifted the lid and looked inside. About two-thirds of the way down was a little door, so I opened it. Inside he had put a purple glass heart.

"That's to remind you that God loves you—and so do I," he said with a big grin.

The box sits in my office, and I often open it, take out that glass heart, and hold it for a moment. Some days I just need to remind myself of God's faithful love. You probably do too.

And when you do, I imagine you pinpoint important milestones in your faith journey, times when God delivered you or clearly spoke a word of comfort.

The Israelites discovered the value of making a pilgrimage to these points along their faith journey. They shared with their children the stories of God's past deliverance as they went about their daily work. They recounted those moments of rescue in their songs and poems. They reenacted them during their festivals.

A glimpse into Jesus' childhood came during one of these communal remembrances of God's faithfulness. You may remember when the young Savior stayed behind in crowded Jerusalem as the others headed home to Nazareth. Did you know that the pilgrimage to Jerusalem—the journey itself—was an occasion for remembering?

As the people walked along the popular Ridge Route, they passed many sites that were important to their faith: Shechem, where the covenant was made; Mount Ebal, where Joshua rededicated Israel as they settled in the promised land; and Bethel, where God made promises to Jacob. As they walked, the parents pointed out these sites and taught their children about God's great faithfulness. The people knew the importance of looking back.

Looking back is important for us too. If you're facing seemingly impossible circumstances today, take a moment to look back and remember when God did the impossible for you. As you thank Him for His past deliverance, you'll find fresh courage for the present challenge.

> *Look back with gratitude and you will look forward with faith.*

❧ Five Minutes in the Word ❧

You shall remember that you were a slave in the land of Egypt, and the LORD your God brought you out from there with a mighty hand and an outstretched arm.

Deuteronomy 5:15

Only take care, and keep your soul diligently, lest you forget the things that your eyes have seen, and lest they depart from your heart all the days of your life. Make them known to your children and your children's children.

Deuteronomy 4:9

You shall teach [God's commands] diligently to your children,
and shall talk of them when you sit in your house, and when you
walk by the way, and when you lie down, and when you rise.

Deuteronomy 6:7

This is what the LORD says: "Stop at the crossroads and look
around. Ask for the old, godly way, and walk in it."

Jeremiah 6:16 NLT

I will remember the deeds of the LORD; yes, I will
remember your miracles of long ago.

Psalm 77:11 NIV

Equipped for the Task at Hand

Elizabeth was born a slave. At the age of eleven, she was taken from her family and sent to a plantation far away. Utterly grief-stricken, she wept constantly and even stopped eating. One night she grew so weak that she was sure she would die. She hardly knew how to pray, but as she cried out to God, a figure cloaked in a brilliant white garment appeared before her. And God placed His call on the most unlikely of servants in pre–Civil War America: a young slave girl.

Elizabeth became a powerful evangelist who preached against the evils of slavery to both black and white congregations. On paper, she was terribly ill-equipped for the task: she had no education; she was a woman in a man's world; and she was black during a time when people of color had no voice. Of course she met doubt and resistance everywhere she went.

But she knew where to go to be equipped for the task to which her Lord had called her: Elizabeth took her needs to Jesus.[6]

This truth could have helped Israel's first king before he was ever crowned. When Saul learned about God's plan for him, he realized the calling was too big: foreign enemies pressed in on Israel's borders; tribes were scheming and jealous; and people had crazy high expectations for their nation's very first king. So when the time for his coronation arrived and the announcement rang, the trumpets blasted, and . . . no Saul.

So they started looking for the king, and they found him—but only after the Lord told them, "He is hiding among the baggage" (1 Samuel 10:22 NLT).

Saul had considered the job description, sized up his own character, and found himself not up to the task.

Saul didn't know that when that happens—when we find ourselves at the end of our own wisdom, courage, and strength—we have only one option: we must lay our inadequacies before the throne of God and allow Him to do His work through us.

When we do, we experience the peace that enables us to crawl out of hiding and into God's purpose for our lives.

> *We serve God well when, in our weakness, we turn to Him for wisdom, courage, and strength.*

⋆⟨ Five Minutes in the Word ⟩⋆

From the end of the earth I will cry to You, when my heart is overwhelmed; lead me to the rock that is higher than I.

Psalm 61:2 NKJV

Have you not known? Have you not heard? The LORD is the everlasting God, the Creator of the ends of the earth. He does not faint or grow weary; his understanding is unsearchable.

Isaiah 40:28

The LORD is my strength and shield. I trust him with all my heart. He helps me, and my heart is filled with joy. I burst out in songs of thanksgiving.

Psalm 28:7 NLT

"I have told you all this so that you may have peace in me. Here on earth you will have many trials and sorrows. But take heart, because I have overcome the world."

John 16:33 NLT

Beautiful Feet

It was Sunday, and I was standing in line for coffee behind two young women. One put her Bible down on the counter, reached into her purse for her wallet, and said, "I just don't watch the news anymore. It's too depressing."

"I know," the other agreed. "I just watch reruns of *The Office*."

I sat in my car for a while thinking about those young women who expressed a sentiment that many share, and it troubled me.

I wondered, *Why do we think we are here at this moment in human history?* It's no accident that, through a multitude of social networking platforms, we now have access to those who are suffering. Some of these issues have existed since the beginning of the human story, but now we know about them.

When God placed our feet on this earth at this time, He did so knowing that the world would be slowly bleeding to death. Some people are crying out for mercy, some for vengeance, and the cries are getting louder. So what can you and I do?

The prophet Isaiah wrote, "How beautiful on the mountains are the feet of the messenger who brings good news, the good news of peace and salvation, the news that the God of Israel reigns!" (Isaiah 52:7 NLT).

What will you and I do in response to that verse? What will we do to take good news to a world often reluctant to receive it?

I think sharing is most effective when we start with what we are personally convinced of, those truths that we would stake our lives on.

When we start every day in Christ's presence and then walk through our days resting in the absolute conviction that no matter what happens, God is in control, we exude a peace that demands an explanation.

People around us live in quiet desperation. Let us live in such a way that our feet will lead them to Jesus.

> *Let our lives light a pathway to peace with You, peace for eternity.*

❧ Five Minutes in the Word ❧

I have not kept the good news of your justice hidden in my heart; I
have talked about your faithfulness and saving power. I have told
everyone in the great assembly of your unfailing love and faithfulness.

Psalm 40:10 NLT

The Lord gives the word; the women who
announce the news are a great host.

Psalm 68:11

Peacemakers who sow in peace reap a harvest of righteousness.

James 3:18 NIV

The message of the cross is foolishness to those who are perishing,
but to us who are being saved it is the power of God.

1 Corinthians 1:18 NIV

As a prisoner for the Lord, then, I urge you to live a
life worthy of the calling you have received.

Ephesians 4:1 NIV

When We Need It

During the Roman persecution of the Jews, Rabbi Akiva was asked why he persisted in teaching God's Word when doing so could mean torture and death. He answered with a parable:

Once as a fox was walking alongside a river, he noticed the fish swimming frantically back and forth, never stopping for rest.

"Why the big hurry?" the fox asked. "What do you have to fear?"

"We're afraid of the fishermen's nets," the fish replied.

"Well, that's an easy problem to solve," said the fox. "Just come live with me up here on the dry land."

The fish laughed: "That's a crazy idea! If we're in danger down here in our element, how much more danger would be in if we abandoned it!"

"It is the same situation for us," Rabbi Akiva explained. "We have been told that God's Word is our very life. If that is true for us in times of peace, how much more do we need it in times such as these?"[7]

When life gets chaotic and difficult, we can be tempted to allow our time with God's Word to slip away, but, as Rabbi Akiva pointed out, that's when we need it the most!

Psalm 119 also teaches and celebrates the importance of God's life-giving Word:

"Your word is a lamp to my feet and a light to my path" (v. 105).

"I lie in the dust; revive me by your word" (v. 25 NLT).

"My soul is weary with sorrow; strengthen me according to your word" (v. 28 NIV).

What about you? If you're discouraged today, if your soul is weary with sorrow, trust that there is no comfort, no encouragement, and no power like that found in the Word of God.

Rabbi Akiva was absolutely right: If God's Word is good for us when times are peaceful, how much *more* do we need it in times like these?

> *God's Word is there when we need it—and we need it now!*

⊱ Five Minutes in the Word ⊰

I delight in your decrees; I will not neglect your word.

Psalm 119:16 NIV

The word of God is alive and active. Sharper than any double-edged sword, it penetrates even to dividing soul and spirit, joints and marrow; it judges the thoughts and attitudes of the heart.

Hebrews 4:12 NIV

Turn my eyes away from worthless things;
preserve my life according to your word.

Psalm 119:37 NIV

The Sovereign LORD has given me his words of wisdom, so that I know how to comfort the weary. Morning by morning he wakens me and opens my understanding to his will.

Isaiah 50:4 NLT

The law of the LORD is perfect, refreshing the soul. The statutes of the LORD are trustworthy, making wise the simple. The precepts of the LORD are right, giving joy to the heart. The commands of the LORD are radiant, giving light to the eyes. The fear of the LORD is pure, enduring forever. The decrees of the LORD are firm, and all of them are righteous. They are more precious than gold, than much pure gold; they are sweeter than honey, than honey from the honeycomb. By them your servant is warned; in keeping them there is great reward.

Psalm 19:7–11 NIV

The Peace of Reconciliation

Morris Brown African Methodist Episcopal (AME) Church was packed. The lower level of the sanctuary had standing room only. The balcony was at capacity too. Those who didn't get a spot inside gathered on the church lawn where volunteers passed out ice water to provide relief from the stifling summer heat.

The mixed race crowd wasn't there to see a world-famous evangelist or a Grammy-winning gospel artist. They had come to mourn and to pray.

Tragedy had just befallen their sister church, Emmanuel AME Church. A young man professing racist ideologies had entered the historical church and taken the lives of nine members who had met to worship and pray.

Now, at Morris Brown AME Church, Christians had gathered to seek God. Black and white brothers and sisters in Christ shed tears together. They held one another's hands and lifted them high in worship. They knelt together in unity before the cross of Christ, living out the truth of Ephesians 2:13–14: "In Christ Jesus you who once were far off have been brought near by the blood of Christ. For he himself is our peace, who has made us both one."[8]

In this letter, Paul was addressing the ethnic crisis of his time: the divide between Jewish Christians and Greek Christians. For hundreds of years, the Jews had lived out a deeply entrenched mentality of exclusion: if you were Jewish, you were in; if you weren't, you were out. Even if a non-Jew took steps toward the one true God, he was kept on the fringe.

So, yes, Paul was saying something revolutionary here. He proclaimed that there is no more "us and them" in the body of Christ-followers, because we are *one* now. And we are one because Jesus died on the cross, taking on the punishment of our sins.

The Hebrew word for *peace* in Ephesians 2:14 is *eirene*, and it means "peace, quietness, rest" as well as "set at one again." *Eirene* is a word of reconciliation and unification.

Because Jesus paid the price for our sins when He died on the cross, we are at peace with God and with one another—no matter our past, no matter our roots, and no matter the color of our skin. In Jesus, we are one. He truly is our peace.

> *Christ is our peace . . . our constant,*
> *unshakable peace.*

✧ Five Minutes in the Word ✧

As many of you as were baptized into Christ have put on Christ.
There is neither Jew nor Greek, there is neither slave nor free, there
is no male and female, for you are all one in Christ Jesus.

Galatians 3:27–28

We pursue the things which make for peace
and the building up of one another.

Romans 14:19 NASB

I appeal to you, brothers, by the name of our Lord Jesus Christ, that
all of you agree, and that there be no divisions among you, but
that you be united in the same mind and the same judgment.

1 Corinthians 1:10

Conduct yourselves in a manner worthy of the gospel of Christ,
so that whether I come and see you or remain absent, I will
hear of you that you are standing firm in one spirit, with
one mind striving together for the faith of the gospel.

Philippians 1:27 NASB

If you have any encouragement from being united with Christ, if
any comfort from his love, if any common sharing in the Spirit, if
any tenderness and compassion, then make my joy complete by
being like-minded, having the same love, being one in spirit and
of one mind. Do nothing out of selfish ambition or vain conceit.
Rather, in humility value others above yourselves, not looking to
your own interests but each of you to the interests of the others.

Philippians 2:1–4 NIV

"Have Mercy on
Me, a Sinner"

Singer extraordinaire Natalie Grant was the one who introduced me to Twitter. One day as we waited to board a plane, she asked me, "Do you tweet?"

I replied, "I hope not." I was clueless.

When Natalie explained what Twitter was, it seemed like just one more way to clutter up our lives. I have since come to value the way it can connect us, especially as we pray for one another. But there is one thing that troubles me about social media: it makes it so easy for us to judge others.

I recently read a post from a young woman who humbly confessed to being an alcoholic. She had lost her sobriety yet again and was asking for prayer. Several people immediately wrote notes of encouragement, but a couple of Pharisees jumped all over her. It was a virtual stoning. When we don't maintain a balance between grace and truth, we quickly become destructive and self-righteous.

Consider Jesus' parable in Luke 18:9–14. A Pharisee (whom people at that time would consider righteous) and a tax collector (considered by most the worst possible sinner) had gone to the temple to pray. The tax collector stood with his head bowed, beating his chest, crying, "God, be merciful to me, a sinner!" (v. 13). The Pharisee's prayer, however, was first a list of all the good things he did and then a list of all the people he considered himself far better than, including the tax collector. The Pharisee had completely missed the heart of God.

Have we?

How do we know when we have strayed from grace and truth? First, we realize that our focus is no longer on God, but rather on the person next to us. Glorifying God is no longer our goal. We merely want to look better than the folks around us.

Second, when we have strayed from grace and truth, peace has usually evaporated, and judgment and self-righteousness have taken its place. We are focused on being good enough for God, and, in our minds, that means being better than others.

If you find yourself lacking mercy today, take a moment to refocus. Take your eyes off your neighbor and gaze instead at the Lover of your soul, the One who will enable you to love others.

> *Jesus loves you just the way you are, and can help you love others just the way they are.*

⤳ Five Minutes in the Word ⤳

As the eyes of servants look to the hand of their master, as the eyes of a maidservant to the hand of her mistress, so our eyes look to the LORD our God, till he has mercy upon us.

Psalm 123:2

To you, LORD, I called; to the LORD I cried for mercy.

Psalm 30:8 NIV

"Do not judge others, and you will not be judged. For you will be treated as you treat others. The standard you use in judging is the standard by which you will be judged."

Matthew 7:1–2 NLT

The prize awaits me—the crown of righteousness, which the Lord, the righteous Judge, will give me on the day of his return. And the prize is not just for me but for all who eagerly look forward to his appearing.

2 Timothy 4:8 NLT

The LORD is our judge, our lawgiver, and our
king. He will care for us and save us.

Isaiah 33:22 NLT

The Tempting Pathway
of the People Pleaser

During the early days of the Nazis' rise to power, many Germans, including Christians, felt optimistic about Adolf Hitler's leadership. Having suffered greatly in the wake of World War I, the people of Germany longed for the days when the nation's glory would be restored. The Nazis seemed to be the answer to these hopes and dreams.

One young theologian, however, saw the nation's politics through a different lens. Dietrich Bonhoeffer sensed in Nazi beliefs a sinister philosophy that was in direct opposition to God's idea of justice. While his Christian brothers imagined the bright dawn of a new Germany, Bonhoeffer saw the gathering storm of the Holocaust on the horizon. The church was simply . . . asleep.

Bonhoeffer knew he had to do something to awaken it before it was too late for the Jews. In the spring of 1933, he carefully prepared an essay to share with a group of pastors, challenging them—challenging the church—to rise up in defense of the Jews.

When Bonhoeffer presented the essay, many pastors walked out before he reached his second point. Yet he knew he had heard God's call to try to awaken the church, and his obedience led to his incarceration in Flossenbürg prison.[9]

Most of us will never endure the kind of suffering this man of God did, but all of us will at some point or other be in a position where choosing to follow God's plan for us makes other people very unhappy.

It is tempting to long for the approval of others, but anytime I allow my desire to please people to influence my decisions, peace goes right out the window! I don't forfeit that calmness, though, when I remember whom I am supposed to please.

Paul put it this way: "Am I now seeking the approval of man, or of God? Or am I trying to please man? If I were still trying to please man, I would not be a servant of Christ" (Galatians 1:10).

None of us can keep everyone happy all the time, but we can live out our tough choices with courage and peace when we remember whom we serve. If we are living to please God, His approval is enough.

⋰ Five Minutes in the Word ⋱

To me to live is Christ, and to die is gain.

Philippians 1:21

If then you have been raised with Christ, seek the things that are above, where Christ is, seated at the right hand of God. Set your minds on things that are above, not on things that are on earth. For you have died, and your life is hidden with Christ in God.

Colossians 3:1–3

My life is worth nothing to me unless I use it for finishing the work assigned me by the Lord Jesus—the work of telling others the Good News about the wonderful grace of God.

Acts 20:24 NLT

Dear brothers and sisters, we urge you in the name of the Lord Jesus to live in a way that pleases God, as we have taught you. You live this way already, and we encourage you to do so even more.

1 Thessalonians 4:1 NLT

We continually ask God to fill you with the knowledge of his will through all the wisdom and understanding that the Spirit gives, so that you may live a life worthy of the Lord and please him in every way: bearing fruit in every good work, growing in the knowledge of God, being strengthened with all power according to his glorious might so that you may have great endurance and patience, and giving joyful thanks to the Father, who has qualified you to share in the inheritance of his holy people in the kingdom of light.

Colossians 1:9–12 NIV

The Reason for Courage

A soft-spoken, gentle man with silver hair, Louis Sako is an archbishop and patriarch of the Chaldean Catholic Church. He recently survived an assassination attempt, but that kind of danger hasn't kept him from ministering in one of the most difficult places on earth, a place where bombs explode and ISIS is on the march. A place where his life is under constant threat. Why does he stay?

"We are consecrated," he has explained. "We gave our lives [to our Lord] . . . we should be courageous."[10]

Our world today can seem especially frightening. How do we live courageously—how can we be the beautiful fragrance of the peace of Christ—in a time when ordinary moments are increasingly invaded by random acts of violence?

In the Old Testament, Gideon faced this same challenge. When we first meet him in Judges 6, he is threshing wheat in a winepress to hide it from the Midianites. For seven years Israel had been suffering terrible oppression under Midian's harsh rule. This enemy moved through the land like locusts, consuming or destroying everything in their path (v. 5). The Israelites had been forced to live in caves to survive.

When the angel of the Lord appeared to commission Gideon to deliver Israel from Midian, their conversation reveals that living under the constant threat of the Midian invaders had taken its toll on Gideon. He was discouraged, insecure, worried, and afraid. It's unthinkable that a man like Gideon could go on to become a mighty warrior, a judge for the nation of Israel—but that's what happened. What made the difference?

The answer to that question is found in Judges 6:22–24. Under a terebinth tree, near the winepress where he had been threshing wheat, a fearful, anxious, traumatized Gideon met with God. That encounter transformed the man.

Gideon built an altar to God on the site to commemorate the moment the power of God changed his life, and he named the altar "The Lord Is Peace" (v. 24).

Has living in our uncertain age stolen your peace? Make time to get alone with God today. Let Him remind you that He is and He always will be—forever and ever—your refuge, your strength, and your peace.

> *Make this truth your primary thought today: the Lord is peace.*

⟫⟨ Five Minutes in the Word ⟩⟨

God is our refuge and strength, a very present help in trouble.
Therefore we will not fear though the earth gives way, though the
mountains be moved into the heart of the sea, though its waters
roar and foam, though the mountains tremble at its swelling.

Psalm 46:1–3

Even if you should suffer for what is right, you are blessed.
"Do not fear their threats; do not be frightened." But in your
hearts revere Christ as Lord. Always be prepared to give an
answer to everyone who asks you to give the reason for the hope
that you have. But do this with gentleness and respect.

1 Peter 3:14–15 NIV

Trust in Him at all times, you people; pour out
your hearts before Him. God is our refuge.

Psalm 62:8 HCSB

Every word of God is pure; He is a shield
to those who take refuge in Him.

Proverbs 30:5 HCSB

We who have fled for refuge might have strong encouragement
to hold fast to the hope set before us. We have [God's
promises] as a sure and steadfast anchor of the soul, a hope
that enters into the inner place behind the curtain.

Hebrews 6:18–19

Give Me Eyes to See

It began with a simple e-mail: "Would you like to meet some of the inmates from the women's prison when you are in town?"

I knew that we had given tickets to about thirty female inmates, a couple guards, and the governor and his wife. We had done that the last few years we'd been in that city, but to get the chance to meet them this time was a gift to us. During the lunch break on Saturday, Jen Hatmaker and I and four of the other speakers from our arena event made our way up to the lounge where the women were gathered.

I wish I could show you their faces. Some, beaten down by life, looked older than their years. Some were surprisingly young and full of possibility. Each of us speakers took a few moments to share what was on our hearts.

We spoke about the relentless love and grace of God.

We spoke about forgiveness and new beginnings.

We spoke about the peace of Christ that can invade the least likely places.

As tears flowed down all our faces, the six of us each gathered a group of the women together and knelt at their feet and prayed for them. Although we were in the Jack Daniel's Lounge (yep, that was the name!), it felt like holy ground. There was no division, no "them" and "us," because it was crystal clear that we were all sinners in need of God's mercy and grace.

Most of the women we met already had a relationship with Christ; two received Him that day. I stayed behind for a while to listen to some of their stories. Many accounts were heartbreaking, but the common thread was very apparent: Christ offers peace in the darkest of moments. I went there praying that Christ might touch the hearts of these women through me. Christ touched my heart through them.

I wonder how often we miss the beauty of what Christ is doing in the life of another person because we don't bother to look past the externals.

This is a daily prayer of mine: *Lord, today give me eyes to see what I would miss without You. Give me ears to hear what's not being said but is the cry of another's heart. Amen.*

> *There is no pit too deep that the peace of Christ cannot reach to the very bottom.*

ꗠ Five Minutes in the Word ꗡ

There is therefore now no condemnation for
those who are in Christ Jesus.

Romans 8:1

I am convinced that nothing can ever separate us from God's love.
Neither death nor life, neither angels nor demons, neither our fears for
today nor our worries about tomorrow—not even the powers of hell can
separate us from God's love. No power in the sky above or in the earth
below—indeed, nothing in all creation will ever be able to separate
us from the love of God that is revealed in Christ Jesus our Lord.

Romans 8:38–39 NLT

The man looked around. "Yes," he said, "I see people, but I can't see
them very clearly. They look like trees walking around." Then Jesus
placed his hands on the man's eyes again, and his eyes were opened.
His sight was completely restored, and he could see everything clearly.

Mark 8:24–25 NLT

Share each other's burdens, and
in this way obey the law of Christ.
Galatians 6:2 NLT

You are helping us by praying for us.
2 Corinthians 1:11 NLT

Trusting God for Enough

In the spring of AD 70, the Romans advanced upon Jerusalem and placed the city under siege. Knowing that the pilgrims would drain the city's food and water supplies, the Romans allowed them to enter Jerusalem for Passover—and then didn't let them leave. Days and weeks stretched into months, and Jerusalem began to starve. Before the siege was lifted, the Jews of Jerusalem even attempted to eat their leather belts and shoes.

By God's grace, few of us will ever be as desperately hungry or fearful as these trapped Jews were. After all, God doesn't want us to live in fear. He wants us to live peacefully in the freedom that comes from trusting Him to provide for us. The Bible is rich with God's promises that He will meet our needs, and one of my favorites is tucked into the words of the Lord's Prayer: "Give us this day our daily bread" (Matthew 6:11).

Have you ever noticed the repetition of *day* and *daily*

in that sentence? New Testament scholar Kenneth Bailey explains that the words are repeated because of the difficult-to-translate Greek word *epiousios*. As a matter of fact, there is no record of this word being used anywhere else in Greek literature. Biblical scholars have translated the word in a handful of ways over the years, but the oldest commentary we have on the subject—and the one most closely related to Aramaic, the language Jesus spoke—is the Old Syriac. That translation is: "Give us today the bread that doesn't run out."[11]

Clearly, Jesus doesn't want us to be anxious about whether we will have what we need in order to live. He encourages us to simply ask God to meet those needs, to ask Him for bread that keeps coming.

What need is weighing on you today? God doesn't want you lying awake at night in worry or fear. He invites you to come to Him and, with trusting, childlike faith, ask Him to provide for you.

> *Thank You, Father, that Your provision for me will never run out.*

✑ Five Minutes in the Word ✑

"Do not be anxious about your life, what you will eat or what you will drink, nor about your body, what you will put on. Is not life more than food, and the body more than clothing? Look at the birds of the air: they neither sow nor reap nor gather into barns, and yet your heavenly Father feeds them. Are you not of more value than they?"

Matthew 6:25–26

I have been young, and now am old, yet I have not seen the righteous forsaken or his children begging for bread. He is ever lending generously, and his children become a blessing.

Psalm 37:25–26

Search me, God, and know my heart; test me and know my anxious thoughts.

Psalm 139:23 NIV

It is useless for you to work so hard from early morning until late at night, anxiously working for food to eat; for God gives rest to his loved ones.

Psalm 127:2 NLT

Treasures in Heaven

Remember the term *Y2K*?

Were you were caught up in the drama and perhaps even the preparation as the world awaited the disaster that would supposedly come at the turn of the century? I wasn't just caught up; I was fully immersed—and not by choice.

My father-in-law, William, and my husband, Barry, were convinced that when clocks struck midnight on January 1, 2000, the world would be unplugged, and we'd all be fumbling around for matches. So they . . . prepared! We had a portable toilet, a shower, a wind-up radio, candles that burn for months, and enough seed to replant America. I have to admit, I did my part: I bought a lot of chocolate. I told them it was for bartering, but I had no intentions of giving it up.

All joking aside, how do we prepare for the future in our very uncertain world?

Jesus offers us this wisdom: "Do not lay up for yourselves treasures on earth, where moth and rust destroy and where thieves break in and steal, but lay up for yourselves treasures in heaven, where neither moth nor rust destroys and where thieves do not break in and steal. For where your treasure is, there your heart will be also" (Matthew 6:19–21).

It isn't bad to have material possessions, but making them the focus of our lives only leads to anxiety and frustration because they are temporal. God wants us to enjoy the rich life of peace that comes from loving Him and what He loves. God wants us to invest our lives in our brothers and sisters in Christ, to extend grace and mercy to the suffering, and to share the good news that, by Christ's death on the cross, we are reconciled to the Father. When these activities are our focus, we store up treasures for ourselves in a place of absolute security: heaven itself.

A peaceful heart is focused on Christ.

❧ Five Minutes in the Word ❧

"Let not your hearts be troubled. Believe in God; believe also
in me. In my Father's house are many rooms. If it were not so,
would I have told you that I go to prepare a place for you? And
if I go and prepare a place for you, I will come again and will
take you to myself, that where I am you may be also."

John 14:1–3

My God will meet all your needs according to
the riches of his glory in Christ Jesus.

Philippians 4:19 NIV

Sing out your thanks to the LORD; sing praises to our God with a
harp. He covers the heavens with clouds, provides rain for the
earth, and makes the grass grow in mountain pastures.

Psalm 147:7–8 NLT

God will generously provide all you need. Then you will always have
everything you need and plenty left over to share with others.

2 Corinthians 9:8 NLT

He has provided food for those who fear Him;
He remembers His covenant forever.

Psalm 111:5 HCSB

An Act of Faith in Our Faithful God

My friend had recently given her life to Christ, and she found everything about her new life fresh and exciting. She was hungry for the Word of God, and every revelation strengthened her faith and increased her passion . . . until we came to the principle of tithing.

"You mean that you give God 10 percent of everything on really good months, when you have cash to spare, right?" she asked.

"No," I said. "As daughters of the King, we give Him 10 percent of our income even in the rough months. It's lining our lives up with the Word of God. It's also our way of saying that we trust God to provide for us."

"Sounds a bit irresponsible," she commented. "Shouldn't I pay all my bills first?"

"If you honor God, He will honor your trust in Him," I reassured her. "He never fails."

"I hope I have enough!" she said.

My friend's struggle is hardly new. The nation of Israel, for instance, seemed especially vulnerable to Baal worship. That idolatry was deeply rooted in the fear that God would not be enough for them.

When captive Israel farmed in Egypt, they counted on the annual flooding of the Nile. When they entered the wilderness and became a nomadic people, God fed them manna. Then, upon entering the promised land, they became farmers once again, but now there wasn't a Nile River. In Canaan, farmers depended on rain. Israel, however, not only learned from the Canaanites the necessary farming skills but also the closely linked idolatry. The Canaanites believed that if they wanted rain for their crops, they needed to keep Baal, the god of fertility, happy.

So every growing season, Israel had to choose: would she depend on God to provide, or would she give in to the fear that He wouldn't be enough and turn to Baal instead?

We can't judge Israel for such doubt. Despite God's faithfulness to us, we sometimes struggle with the gnawing fear that God won't follow through on His promises, that somehow He won't be enough.

Our God is faithful. Don't allow fear to deceive you. Trust your heavenly Father to provide for your needs today, and you'll know His sweet peace as well.

> *Honor God in all your ways,*
> *knowing that He will take care of you.*

⤳ Five Minutes in the Word ⤲

"If you will indeed obey my commandments that I command you today,
*to love the L*ORD *your God, and to serve him with all your heart and*
with all your soul, he will give the rain for your land in its season, the
early rain and the later rain, that you may gather in your grain and
your wine and your oil. And he will give grass in your fields for your
livestock, and you shall eat and be full. Take care lest your heart be
deceived, and you turn aside and serve other gods and worship them."

Deuteronomy 11:13–16

He is the Maker of heaven and earth, the sea, and everything
in them—he remains faithful forever. He upholds the
cause of the oppressed and gives food to the hungry.

Psalm 146:6–7 NIV

All the ways of the LORD are loving and faithful toward those who keep the demands of his covenant.

Psalm 25:10 NIV

If any of you lacks wisdom, let him ask God, who gives generously to all without reproach, and it will be given him.

James 1:5

God is able to make all grace abound to you, so that having all sufficiency in all things at all times, you may abound in every good work.

2 Corinthians 9:8

Learning How to
Shut the Door

Have you noticed what people these days do when they're in line at the grocery store, waiting for their turn at a gas pump, or sitting in an auditorium ready for the curtain to rise? Most of them are looking at their smartphones—checking e-mail, getting an update on their favorite team, playing a game, ordering dinner, texting a friend. We fill not only our empty moments with our phones, but often the time we're with other people as well. ("No phones at the dinner table!" is now a parent's common cry.) Smartphones usually mean less person-to-person, heart-to-heart interaction.

And if we're finding little time to invest in relationships with people, we're probably also struggling to find time for God, time to listen for His voice of comfort, love, guidance, and peace.

God speaks quietly. Do we have any stillness in our lives where we wait for Him and listen for His voice?

Listen to the words of Psalm 130:5–6: "I wait for the LORD, my soul waits, and in his word I hope; my soul waits for the Lord more than watchmen for the morning, more than watchmen for the morning."

I want that to be the cry of my heart! I want God's words to me to be so precious that I hunger for time with Him more than anything else in my life. If I am going to hear His voice, I need to make space in my days.

Oh, it is easy to make excuses about being too busy, but whenever I try to justify my packed schedule, something deep inside me whispers that I make time for what I value the most. Oswald Chambers, who was never one to mince words, had this to say about my excuses: "It is *so* difficult to get 'quiet,' you say. . . . Oh, it can be done, but you must know how to shut the door."[12]

So, the next time I have some free moments, I think I'll do something countercultural. I am going to turn off my phone, be quiet, and listen for God to speak. It is time to learn how to "shut the door" on distractions and open my heart to God.

> *Speak, Lord, for I am listening.*

⸒⸒ Five Minutes in the Word ⸒⸒

*Eli told Samuel, "Go and lie down, and if he calls you, say, 'Speak, Lord,
for your servant is listening.'" So Samuel went and lay down in his place.*

1 Samuel 3:9 NIV

*Show us your steadfast love, O Lord, and grant us your salvation. Let me
hear what God the Lord will speak, for he will speak peace to his people,
to his saints; but let them not turn back to folly. Surely his salvation
is near to those who fear him, that glory may dwell in our land.*

Psalm 85:7–9

*I have calmed and quieted my soul, like a weaned child with
its mother; like a weaned child is my soul within me.*

Psalm 131:2

Let all that I am wait quietly before God, for my hope is in him.

Psalm 62:5 NLT

*This is what the Sovereign Lord, the Holy One of Israel,
says: "Only in returning to me and resting in me will you be
saved. In quietness and confidence is your strength."*

Isaiah 30:15 NLT

A Day of Rest and Peace

It had been a crazy day. Actually, it had been a crazy week. I'd returned from a trip to a pile of laundry the size of Texas, an empty refrigerator, and a hungry teenager and his five friends. After rustling up a pasta dish, I got the first load of whites into the washer and fed the dogs. Checking my e-mail I discovered that I had missed a deadline for a magazine article, but they were willing to extend it if I could get it to them by morning. And there were three notes by the phone:

"Call your mom."

"Call the vet."

"Call the radio station. You missed an interview this morning."

I was ready to get on a slow boat to China!

We all live crazy lives, but they become unmanageable when we forget to honor one of God's commands: our heavenly Father—the King of kings—our Creator—wants us to keep the Sabbath. Maybe we should pay attention!

The word *Sabbath* (*shabbot* in Hebrew) means "to desist from exertion, to cease, to celebrate, to rest, to be still." God modeled this ceasing from exertion when, after six days of creating, He chose to rest on the seventh. The Sabbath is a time to pause in our work, slow down, and be still. It is a day to worship God and listen for His voice. The Sabbath enables us to enter our God-given work with renewed energy and purpose. When we have sabbathed with God, we bring His life into our work.

In his beautiful book *Christ Plays in Ten Thousand Places*, Eugene Peterson warns us of the perils of working without having received God's gift of the Sabbath: "Without Sabbath . . . the workplace is soon emptied of any sense of the presence of God and the work becomes an end in itself. It is this 'end in itself' that makes an un-sabbathed workplace a breeding ground for idols. We make idols in our workplaces when we reduce all relationships to functions we can manage. We make idols in our workplace when we reduce work to the dimensions of our egos and control."[13]

How miserable does that sound? No wonder people snap!

I don't know about you, but I don't want work that is empty of God. I want to go about my daily tasks, no matter how mundane, filled with the Spirit and doing all for the glory of Christ.

So I take time to stop, listen, and rest. On the Sabbath, I aim to empty my hands and heart of all except worship. I find a rich sense of peace that day, and I carry it into my week. Or maybe it carries me!

> *"Be still and know that I am God."*

✒ Five Minutes in the Word ✒

By the seventh day God had finished the work he had been doing; so on the seventh day he rested from all his work. Then God blessed the seventh day and made it holy, because on it he rested from all the work of creating that he had done.

Genesis 2:2–3 NIV

No working on the Sabbath; keep it holy just as GOD, your God, commanded you. Work six days, doing everything you have to do, but the seventh day is a Sabbath, a Rest Day—no work; not you, your son, your daughter, your servant, your maid, your ox, your donkey (or any of your animals), and not even the foreigner visiting your town. That way your servants and maids will get the same rest as you.

Deuteronomy 5:12–14 THE MESSAGE

The Lord is my shepherd; I have all that I need. He lets me rest in green meadows; he leads me beside peaceful streams. He renews my strength.

Psalm 23:1–3 NLT

Those who live in the shelter of the Most High will find rest in the shadow of the Almighty.

Psalm 91:1 NLT

"Come to me, all who labor and are heavy laden, and I will give you rest. Take my yoke upon you, and learn from me, for I am gentle and lowly in heart, and you will find rest for your souls."

Matthew 11:28–29

Lift Your Voice in Praise!

As the crane plucked the cross from the top of Yahui Church in Pingyang County, Wenzhou City, China, Christians cried out in dismay and began weeping. But then their tremulous voices, ragged with tears, erupted in spontaneous praise.

"Cross, cross, be my glory forever!" and "All my sins have been washed away by the blood of Jesus" were some of the believers' cries.[14]

In recent months, the Chinese government has intensified its persecution of Christians, frequently targeting their places of worship and demolishing churches. In many other incidences, crosses are forcibly removed from the tops of church buildings.

My heart grieves for our brothers and sisters in China even as I stand in holy awe that such suffering is a catalyst for spontaneous praise.

Christians have long found solace and hope in songs

of praise even during desperate times. Remember, for instance, Paul and Silas. They were shackled in prison, their bodies bruised and bloodied from their recent beating, and even though it was midnight, they weren't sleeping.

Instead, they were "praying and singing hymns to God, and the prisoners were listening to them" (Acts 16:25). The brilliant light of praise shot through that dark moment of suffering, and God changed everything.

Scripture tells us He sent an earthquake so violent that the prison doors were thrown open and shackles fell from the prisoners. This act of God's power and glory compelled Paul and Silas's jailer and his entire family to become believers.

Is your heart weighed down by sorrow today? Take a moment to lift your voice—however tremulous it is, however ragged with tears—and praise your God. Praise lifts our eyes above the darkness and reminds us of such unchangeable truths as God is in control and He loves us. Even during our darkest midnight hours, we are safe in the palm of His hand. And we can know peace.

> *Cross, cross, be my glory forever*
> *and always my reason to praise You!*

ᕯᑄ Five Minutes in the Word ᕲᕬ

The Lord is my strength and my shield; in him my heart trusts, and I
am helped; my heart exults, and with my song I give thanks to him.

Psalm 28:7

"Fear not, for I am with you; be not dismayed, for I am
your God; I will strengthen you, I will help you, I will
uphold you with my righteous right hand."

Isaiah 41:10

Why are you cast down, O my soul, and why are
you in turmoil within me? Hope in God; for I shall
again praise him, my salvation and my God.

Psalm 42:5–6

The Lord is my strength and my defense; he has become my salvation. He
is my God, and I will praise him, my father's God, and I will exalt him.

Exodus 15:2 NIV

Let all who take refuge in you rejoice; let them sing joyful
praises forever. Spread your protection over them, that
all who love your name may be filled with joy.

Psalm 5:11 NLT

Finding Peace
Through Purpose

No one would have thought Louis Zamperini would become an Olympic athlete or an American military hero. As a young man, he preferred investing his time and energy in mischief and petty larceny. Then one day a police officer suggested to Louis that he use his speed on the track rather than to avoid arrest.

The seed was sown. In time, something inside Louis changed. He decided he would rather suffer for something that mattered. The book and movie *Unbroken* captured Louis's newfound grit and determination: "If I can take it, I can make it."[15]

He lived out that determination as an Olympic athlete (yes, in track), but this fortitude would carry him through far more difficult trials. When Louis was a young airman in World War II, his plane crashed, leaving him adrift at sea for a staggering forty-seven days until he was finally rescued . . . by the Japanese. Louis spent the remainder of the war in POW camps where he suffered unspeakable abuse.

One secret of his survival was the purpose he and his fellow captives found in their suffering. Working together, they constantly strategized even the smallest ways they could continue fighting the enemy, including stealing rations and gathering intelligence. They were behind bars, true, but they were still soldiers. They would fight however they could.[16]

Louis's story illustrates that we human beings can endure great suffering as long as we know it isn't pointless. We need to know that the hard things we endure are purposeful, that something good will come of them.

What amazing peace comes when we realize that hard things are always purposeful for God's children. God's healing touch transforms every heartbreak and trial for our good and His glory.

Listen to the words of Romans 5:3–5 from *The Message*: "We continue to shout our praise even when we're hemmed in with troubles, because we know how troubles can develop passionate patience in us, and how that patience in turn forges the tempered steel of virtue, keeping us alert for whatever God will do next."

The redemptive touch of Christ transforms our troubles into "passionate patience," virtue as strong as steel, and a heart expecting God to act.

> *Resting in the purpose God*
> *has for you brings peace.*

❧ Five Minutes in the Word ❧

In all this you greatly rejoice, though now for a little while you
may have had to suffer grief in all kinds of trials. These have come
so that the proven genuineness of your faith—of greater worth
than gold, which perishes even though refined by fire—may result
in praise, glory and honor when Jesus Christ is revealed.

1 Peter 1:6–7 NIV

The Holy Spirit helps us in our weakness. For example, we don't
know what God wants us to pray for. But the Holy Spirit prays for us
with groanings that cannot be expressed in words. And the Father
who knows all hearts knows what the Spirit is saying, for the Spirit
pleads for us believers in harmony with God's own will. And we know
that God causes everything to work together for the good of those
who love God and are called according to his purpose for them.

Romans 8:26–28 NLT

I am convinced that nothing can

ever separate us from God's love.

Romans 8:38 NLT

Even though I walk through the valley of the shadow

of death, I will fear no evil, for you are with me;

your rod and your staff, they comfort me.

Psalm 23:4

Peace Before Dawn Breaks

There are several things I find hard to live with, and most of them involve waiting. I don't always wait well. I can take bad news and good news, but I'm not a fan of no news.

Knowing that our son, Christian, would be heading off to college ($$$) in 2015, Barry and I decided to sell our home and move into a smaller one. We'd purchased a larger house when Barry's dad moved in with us, but after his death and now with our one and only beginning a new phase of life, it was time to downsize.

The process of selling a home here in the US is very different from that in my homeland of Scotland. There, if your home is on the market, you welcome prospective buyers, make them a cup of tea, and remain available to answer any questions. Not in America. Our realtor made it clear that we had to clear out—and before we did, hide as many personal items as possible.

"We do still live here, you know," I told her.

"I know that," she said, "but it doesn't have to look like you do."

So every time there was a showing, I had to make a mad dash to remove all signs of life. We had a problem, though. Actually, we had three problems, each with four legs: the dogs. She suggested we put them in the laundry room, so I put a sign on the door: "Do not open. Dogs in here doing laundry."

The trying-to-sell-the-house process has gone on for months with never-ending feedback.

"It's too big."

"It's too small."

"You have too many walls." (That was my favorite.)

As I write, we have an offer, but I have learned that until the ink is dry on the contract, nothing is for sure.

How do you live in the waiting times in your life?

What happens inside of you when you have prayed and prayed about something and don't yet seem to see God working?

Perhaps you're waiting for the result of a medical test. Can you know Christ's peace before you know the results?

When it feels like midnight in your soul, how do you wait until dawn breaks?

At this point in my life, I am learning to worship in the waiting room knowing that—whatever comes—Christ will be there.

> *When we learn to worship in the waiting room, we find peace in His presence.*

⋙ Five Minutes in the Word ⋘

*Wait for the L*ORD*; be strong, and let your heart take courage; wait for the L*ORD*!*

Psalm 27:14

*I wait for your salvation, O L*ORD*.*

Genesis 49:18

*Listen to my voice in the morning, L*ORD*. Each morning I bring my requests to you and wait expectantly.*

Psalm 5:3 NLT

*I waited patiently for the L*ORD *to help me, and he turned to me and heard my cry.*

Psalm 40:1 NLT

There is a special rest still waiting for the people of God.

Hebrews 4:9 NLT

A Holy Wonder

D r. Martin Luther King Jr. had been sentenced to solitary confinement in the Birmingham city jail. Each morning, through the high window of his narrow cell, a few rays of sunlight would enter strong . . . only to be swallowed up by the inky midnight below.

He had been in jail before, but this time was different. This time he was kept in complete isolation. And this time his mind and heart were filled with anxious questions: *What was happening to the movement in his absence? Had bail money been raised for the others who had been arrested? And how were his wife and their baby?* Coretta had given birth only a few days before, and he hadn't even been allowed a telephone call to assure her of his well-being.

Dr. King endured many trials in his pursuit of freedom and justice for African Americans. His writings reveal not only the moments when he broke under the weight of the cause but also the fact that he knew exactly where to turn at those times.

He found renewed strength and peace when he went down on his knees in prayer: "Lord, I must confess that I'm weak now, I'm faltering. I'm losing my courage. Now, I'm afraid."[17]

That prayer shows that Dr. King knew the power of prayer, its ability like beams of light to overcome the inky darkness of our prison cells of doubt, anxiety, and heartache. Prayer makes a difference.

As James wrote in the New Testament, "The prayer of a righteous person is powerful and effective" (James 5:16 NIV).

And isn't that amazing? And mysterious? What a privilege . . . and what a holy wonder! The almighty God of the universe chooses to accomplish His purposes through the prayers of ordinary people like you and me. Our prayers matter: God hears and responds.

Are you weary today? Are you "faltering . . . losing courage . . . afraid"? Are you in the dark?

Turn to God in prayer.

> *God's unfathomable peace and strength await you when you pray.*

✺ Five Minutes in the Word ✺

Cast all your anxiety on him because he cares for you.

1 Peter 5:7 NIV

*Rejoice in the Lord always; again I will say, rejoice. Let your reasonableness
be known to everyone. The Lord is at hand; do not be anxious about anything,
but in everything by prayer and supplication with thanksgiving let your
requests be made known to God. And the peace of God, which surpasses all
understanding, will guard your hearts and your minds in Christ Jesus.*

Philippians 4:4–7

*LORD, I cry out to You; make haste to me! Give ear to my voice
when I cry out to You. Let my prayer be set before You as incense,
the lifting up of my hands as the evening sacrifice.*

Psalm 141:1–2 NKJV

*They cried to the LORD in their trouble, and he delivered them from their distress.
He made the storm be still, and the waves of the sea were hushed. Then they were
glad that the waters were quiet, and he brought them to their desired haven.*

Psalm 107:28–30

*Cast your cares on the LORD and he will sustain you;
he will never let the righteous be shaken.*

Psalm 55:22 NIV

Hold On to Truth

It was the end of summer in Dallas, Texas, and still ridiculously hot. Scottish women are not genetically prepared for Texas heat. I had several errands to run that day, and the last one took me to my doctor's office to pick up a prescription.

As I waited for the elevator, I found myself admiring the woman standing in front of me. She was wearing a beautiful sleeveless top and had the kind of sleek, toned arms and shoulders I've always wanted. (My arms are fine, but they don't have the definition I'd like, so I rarely expose them to the world.) The elevator doors opened, and I pressed the button for the third floor of the parking garage. She pressed the button for the fourth floor.

We stood silently for a few seconds. Then I said to her, "You have such lovely, slender shoulders and arms!"

She turned and looked at me and said, "Thank you. It's cancer."

For a moment I said nothing. Then I said, "I am so sorry!"

She smiled and said, "Hey, it's OK. I'm still here."

The door opened at my floor, and I stepped out. I made my way to my car and got in. I sat for twenty minutes before I could get the tears to stop flowing so that I could drive home. I prayed for her for healing. I prayed that she would find the peace that is found in Christ alone. I felt so shaken and shallow. It's not that my comments were unkind, but they showed me something about myself that I want to pay attention to.

In that elevator I was quick to get caught up in appearances. We live in an image-obsessed world, and images can be misleading, if not deceptive. Without God's help, we will forget there is much more to reality than what meets the eye.

When the apostle Paul wrote to the church in Philippi, he said, "Dear brothers and sisters, one final thing. Fix your thoughts on what is true, and honorable, and right, and pure, and lovely, and admirable. Think about things that are excellent and worthy of praise" (Philippians 4:8 NLT).

There is no greater peace-robber than when we compare ourselves to one another or criticize what we see in the mirror.

The truth that you must hold on to is that you are loved, you are beautiful, you are treasured, and you are a daughter of the Most High God!

> *I am a daughter of the King of kings!*

ᕳᕲ Five Minutes in the Word ᕲᕳ

I praise you because I am fearfully and wonderfully made;
your works are wonderful, I know that full well.

Psalm 139:14 NIV

"Do not consider his appearance or his height, for I have rejected
him. The LORD does not look at the things people look at. People look
at the outward appearance, but the LORD looks at the heart."

1 Samuel 16:7 NIV

Love is patient and kind. Love is not jealous or boastful or proud or rude.
1 Corinthians 13:4–5 NLT

Physical training is of some value, but godliness has value for all
things, holding promise for both the present life and the life to come.

1 Timothy 4:8 NIV

Search me, O God, and know my heart; test me and know
my anxious thoughts. Point out anything in me that offends
you, and lead me along the path of everlasting life.

Psalm 139:23–24 NLT

God Is King

In the most heart-stopping scene of *The Perfect Storm*, fisherman Bobby Shatford turns to Captain Billy Tyne as the sun breaks through the clouds to illuminate the interior of their hurricane-battered fishing boat and says, "We're gonna make it."

The captain looks toward the horizon and surveys the sea as the clouds once again hide the sun. He shakes his head and says, "She's not gonna let us out."

Moments later an immense wave—a mountain of water—rises above their boat, the *Andrea Gail*. Both men furiously work to sail the boat to the top of the wave before it crashes down on top of them.

At that moment the ocean seems monstrous, almost . . . alive.[18]

The ancient Israelites who were following Moses out of Egypt might have described their encounter with the sea in the same way. Not a seafaring people, they found the sea dangerous and foreboding. In time, the image of the seas came to symbolize chaos and evil. No wonder we find joyful proclamations throughout the Old Testament that God is greater than the waters: "The Lord sits enthroned over the flood; the Lord is enthroned as King forever. The Lord gives strength to his people; the Lord blesses his people with peace" (Psalm 29:10–11 NIV).

Isn't that wonderful news? No matter what you face today, whatever the chaos swirling around you, even if the problems before you seem as massive and terrifying as the waves that rose up around the *Andrea Gail*, the chaos and the waves are never too much for God to handle.

Your almighty God is King over all. As a matter of fact, as another psalm proclaims, our powerful God "gathers the waters of the sea into jars; he puts the deep into storehouses" (Psalm 33:7 NIV). Whatever you are facing today, take it to the One who not only loves you but also holds the very seas of the world—and all your problems too—in the palm of His hand.

> *No matter how big the storm, God is bigger.*

༄ Five Minutes in the Word ༄

*"Who shut up the sea behind doors when it burst forth from
the womb, when I made the clouds its garment and wrapped
it in thick darkness, when I fixed limits for it and set its
doors and bars in place, when I said, 'This far you may come
and no farther; here is where your proud waves halt'?"*

Job 38:8–11 NIV

*He stilled the storm to a whisper; the waves of the sea were hushed.
They were glad when it grew calm, and he guided them to their
desired haven. Let them give thanks to the Lᴏʀᴅ for his unfailing love
and his wonderful deeds for mankind. Let them exalt him in the
assembly of the people and praise him in the council of the elders.*

Psalm 107:29–32 NIV

*When Jesus woke up, he rebuked the wind and
said to the waves, "Silence! Be still!" Suddenly the
wind stopped, and there was a great calm.*

Mark 4:39 NLT

*You are a tower of refuge to the poor, O Lᴏʀᴅ, a tower
of refuge to the needy in distress. You are a refuge
from the storm and a shelter from the heat.*

Isaiah 25:4 NLT

*"Have I not commanded you? Be strong and courageous. Do not be frightened, and do not be dismayed, for the L*ORD *your God is with you wherever you go."*

Joshua 1:9

You Have Never Gone This Way Before

Everything they had ever known was about to change forever.

These adults had been children when God commanded their parents to wander in the desert for forty years. They had grown up moving whenever the cloud that symbolized God's presence moved, and making camp whenever and wherever it stopped.

And Moses had always been their leader. He had parted the Red Sea. He had found water for them when they were thirsty, he had mediated their disputes, and he had spoken to God on their behalf.

Forty years had passed. Moses had died, and their parents were all gone too. The wandering children were now adults who, under Joshua's leadership, would enter the promised land.

God was fulfilling the promise He had made to their father Abraham so long ago. The land of Canaan would be theirs; Israel was going home at last. But God had no plans to simply serve up Canaan on a silver platter. He expected them to win it, with His help, through conquest and obedience.

It must have been both exhilarating and terrifying for the people of Israel as they made their way toward their promised home. They knew they would need to cross the Jordan River, which was at flood stage, and then conquer the mighty city of Jericho. Both were formidable tasks, and at first God didn't give any details about just how His people were going to accomplish them. God simply told them to follow the ark of the covenant: "Then you will know which way to go, since you have never been this way before" (Joshua 3:4 NIV).

You see, the ark of the covenant represented the *very presence of God* with the people of Israel, and His presence was enough. Enough to guide them. Enough to keep them safe. Enough to comfort their hearts with assurance and peace as, time and again, they undertook the impossible.

God's presence in our lives is always, *always* enough.

So whatever is before you today—whether it is the same weary stretch of wilderness or the exciting but slightly terrifying unknown— draw near to your Father's side. Let your heart find peace in the promise that He will faithfully guide and protect you on the journey.

> *You've never gone this way before,*
> *but God goes with you.*

ᰀ Five Minutes in the Word ᰀ

The fruit of the Spirit is love, joy, peace, forbearance,
kindness, goodness, faithfulness, gentleness and self-
control. Against such things there is no law.

Galatians 5:22–23 NIV

Those who are led by the Spirit of God are the children of God. The
Spirit you received does not make you slaves, so that you live in fear
again; rather, the Spirit you received brought about your adoption to
sonship. And by him we cry, "Abba, Father." The Spirit himself testifies
with our spirit that we are God's children. Now if we are children,
then we are heirs—heirs of God and co-heirs with Christ, if indeed we
share in his sufferings in order that we may also share in his glory.

Romans 8:14–17 NIV

The Lord says, "I will guide you along the best pathway
for your life. I will advise you and watch over you."

Psalm 32:8 NLT

The Lord will guide you always; he will satisfy your needs in a
sun-scorched land and will strengthen your frame. You will be like
a well-watered garden, like a spring whose waters never fail.

Isaiah 58:11 NIV

Make me to know your ways, O Lord; teach me your paths.
Lead me in your truth and teach me, for you are the God
of my salvation; for you I wait all the day long.

Psalm 25:4–5

Who's in Charge?

He would check into expensive hotels only to sneak out without paying his bill. He never hesitated to steal what he wanted. And he loved to gamble. But when he met Jesus, everything changed.

He was George Müller, a nineteenth-century British evangelist who opened an orphanage in 1836, providing a home for 26 orphans; by 1870 he had 1,722 children living in five different houses. During these years, George trusted God to provide. George never asked for financial support for his efforts or donations of food for the children. Instead, he prayed.

One morning he set the table for breakfast knowing he had absolutely nothing to feed the children. Bowing their heads over empty bowls, George prayed and asked God for their daily bread.

Suddenly, a knock came at the door. The baker explained that he'd been urgently impressed by God to take the children bread. Then the milkman knocked at the door. His cart had broken down in front of the orphanage. He hoped to give his milk to the children so he could unload his cart and repair it. George knew beyond all doubt that God was the source of his provision.[19]

In Judges 6:36–40, we find Gideon attempting to convince himself of this truth. Wanting to confirm that God would be with him as he battled followers of Baal, Gideon asked God to show that He controls the dew.

The test was significant because Israel's enemy served Baal, believing that he controlled the dew and the rain and therefore the success of the crops. Gideon needed to know who was actually in charge: God or Baal. If God proved He had control over the dew, Gideon would be convinced of God's power and strengthened in his resolve to lead the Israelites into battle. If the God who was in charge was with him, he could face anything with courage and peace.

What about you today? Do you believe that God is in charge? He controls the dew . . . the rain . . . and everything else that comes our way.

> *God is in control, and He loves you.*

❧ Five Minutes in the Word ❧

*"If you follow my decrees and are careful to obey my commands, I
will send you rain in its season, and the ground will yield its crops
and the trees their fruit. Your threshing will continue until grape
harvest and the grape harvest will continue until planting, and you
will eat all the food you want and live in safety in your land."*

Leviticus 26:3–5 NIV

*The young lions suffer want and hunger; but those
who seek the LORD lack no good thing.*

Psalm 34:10

*When the LORD your God brings you into the land he swore to your
fathers, to Abraham, Isaac and Jacob, to give you—a land with
large, flourishing cities you did not build, houses filled with all
kinds of good things you did not provide, wells you did not dig,
and vineyards and olive groves you did not plant—then when
you eat and are satisfied, be careful that you do not forget the
LORD, who brought you out of Egypt, out of the land of slavery.*

Deuteronomy 6:10–12 NIV

"Look at the birds of the air: they neither sow nor reap nor gather into barns, and yet your heavenly Father feeds them. Are you not of more value than they? And which of you by being anxious can add a single hour to his span of life? And why are you anxious about clothing? Consider the lilies of the field, how they grow: they neither toil nor spin, yet I tell you, even Solomon in all his glory was not arrayed like one of these."

Matthew 6:26–29

My God will supply every need of yours according to his riches in glory in Christ Jesus.

Philippians 4:19

My Times Are in Your Hands

Although I often talk to my Scottish mom on the phone, I do miss seeing her face. There's just something about the way she smiles and the way she leans in and listens that the phone simply can't capture. I've offered to buy her a computer so that I could send her photos and we could Skype, but she is very suspicious of such modern inventions and refuses to have one in her house. So I came up with plan B.

Every Thursday night Mom has dinner with my sister, so I asked Frances if she would set up a Skype session and surprise Mom. Understatement of the year! Frances had Mom all settled in a chair by the fire, then she brought the computer over and I got to say, "Hi, Mom!" It took her a few minutes to recover, but after that we had a lovely conversation.

A couple hours later, when I knew Mom would be home, I called just to make sure she was settled for the night and ask her if she'd enjoyed our conversation. She said, "Well, I did—but if I'd known I was going to be on television, I would have combed my hair!"

My mom is so precious to me, and it's hard to see her getting old. As sharp as she still is—and I'm thankful for that—so many memories are now on shelves too high for her to reach.

What comfort I find in Psalm 31:14–15: "I trust in you, O LORD; I say, 'You are my God.' My times are in your hand."

My times . . . our times . . . our days, our months, the swiftly passing years, are in our loving Father's hands. He has promised to walk through every minute of them with us, never to leave us or forsake us.

Embracing this truth will not slow the passage of time. Days will still slip by. Even years and decades slip by!

Yet we can know comfort and peace despite the passing of time when we rest in the truth that our God is ever near, speaking words of redemption and reassurance:

"Yes, you made a mistake there, but look how you've grown!"

"Sure, that dream may elude you, but we aren't finished yet."

"I know you missed that opportunity, but I have plans for you that are better than you can imagine."

"I understand it's hard for you to see the seasons pass so quickly. But don't fear: I will stay with you each step of the way."

> *I am so thankful my times are in the hands of my almighty and all-loving heavenly Father.*

༒ Five Minutes in the Word ༒

"Fear not, for I am with you; be not dismayed, for I am your God; I will strengthen you, I will help you. I will uphold you with my righteous right hand."

Isaiah 41:10

"Go therefore and make disciples of all nations, baptizing them in the name of the Father and of the Son and of the Holy Spirit, teaching them to observe all that I have commanded you. And behold, I am with you always, to the end of the age."

Matthew 28:19–20

Be strong and courageous. Do not be afraid or terrified because of them, for the Lord your God goes with you; he will never leave you nor forsake you.

Deuteronomy 31:6 NIV

You saw me before I was born. Every day of my life was recorded in your book. Every moment was laid out before a single day had passed.

Psalm 139:16 NLT

I trust in you, Lord; I say, "You are my God." My times are in your hands.

Psalm 31:14–15 NIV

God's Providence

In the autumn of 1785, Thomas Coke boarded a ship to accompany a group of missionaries to Nova Scotia. From the start, the ship was assaulted by one fierce storm after another. The one-month journey stretched into three, and they never did arrive in Nova Scotia. Ultimately, on Christmas Day, the ship hobbled into the first safe port they found . . . on the island of Antigua.

Thomas knew the name of one man living on the island, a missionary named John Baxter. After Thomas and his fellow missionaries disembarked, they stopped the first person they saw to ask if he knew Mr. Baxter—and it was John Baxter himself on his way to church! The appearance of these fellow missionaries seemed like a gift. By the end of the day's services, Thomas knew they had come to Antigua by the providential hand of God. So there they stayed and saw thousands come to Christ.[20]

The book of Ruth tells another remarkable story of

God's providence. Naomi's husband and sons had died, so she was returning home to Bethlehem with only her daughter-in-law Ruth. Without a male in the family, Ruth needed to provide for the two of them. As she gleaned in the barley fields, Scripture tells us she "happened" to enter the field of a man named Boaz (Ruth 2:3 NKJV).

Boaz was not only a kind and righteous man but also Naomi and Ruth's kinsman-redeemer, a close relative who, in the case of the untimely death of a male heir, would buy that family's land and marry his widow so that the family name might endure.

That is exactly what Boaz did for Ruth, and in doing so, he gave Ruth and Naomi the love and security they so desperately needed.

Sometimes everything in life seems to be going inexplicably wrong. That's when we most need to remember that our lives are—and always will be—in God's hands and that we can trust His providence to lead us safely home.

> *You can worship in the storm,*
> *for God is watching over you.*

✥ Five Minutes in the Word ✥

He strengthens the bars of your gates and blesses your
people within you. He grants peace to your borders
and satisfies you with the finest of wheat.

Psalm 147:13–14 NIV

Good and upright is the LORD; therefore he instructs sinners in
his ways. He guides the humble in what is right and teaches
them his way. All the ways of the LORD are loving and faithful
toward those who keep the demands of his covenant.

Psalm 25:8–10 NIV

The LORD is my light and my salvation—whom shall I fear? The
LORD is the stronghold of my life—of whom shall I be afraid?

Psalm 27:1 NIV

The angel of the LORD encamps around those
who fear him, and he delivers them.

Psalm 34:7 NIV

I Will Not Fear

Allen Emery was in the wool business, and once when he was on a business trip, he actually spent the night in the fields with a shepherd and his flock. When the frightening howls of wolves filled the air, the shepherd's dogs growled, the sheep stirred anxiously, and the shepherd threw some more wood on the fire. When the flames leapt up, Mr. Emery saw thousands of points of lights in the field beyond him. He was surprised to realize that he was seeing the eyes of the sheep: each one turned not toward the danger that threatened them, but toward the source of their protection, the shepherd.[21]

The Twenty-third Psalm, the most beloved and well-known in the psalter, is rich with imagery of a good shepherd's care for his sheep. Verse 4 says, "Even though I walk through the valley of the shadow of death, I will fear no evil, for you are with me; your rod and your staff, they comfort me."

The "valley of the shadow of death" was not simply

allegorical for the psalmist. That phrase referred to a very real place in Israel, known as the Wadi Qelt today. The Wadi Qelt is a deep ravine along the travel route between Jericho and Jerusalem. In antiquity, it was notoriously dangerous, pocketed with bandits and, like many wadis in Israel, prone to flash flooding. (This treacherous route was most likely the setting for Jesus' parable about the good Samaritan.) Is it any wonder the Wadi Qelt earned the nickname "The Valley of the Shadow of Death"?

But the psalmist said that even when he travels through this, the most dangerous of places, he does not fear because his Good Shepherd is always with him. The psalmist proclaimed that, although he faced very real and imminent dangers, his heart was at peace: he knew his loving Shepherd would keep him safe.

Like the sheep Mr. Emery saw, the psalmist kept his eyes not on the dangers all around but on his Shepherd, the source of his protection.

Where is your focus today? On the terrors that stalk you, or the only One who has the power to save you?

> *Keep your eyes on the Good Shepherd,*
> *and your heart will be at peace.*

꒰ Five Minutes in the Word ꒱

"I am the good shepherd. The good shepherd lays down his life for the sheep. He who is a hired hand and not a shepherd, who does not own the sheep, sees the wolf coming and leaves the sheep and flees, and the wolf snatches them and scatters them. He flees because he is a hired hand and cares nothing for the sheep. I am the good shepherd. I know my own and my own know me, just as the Father knows me and I know the Father; and I lay down my life for the sheep."

John 10:11–15

When [Jesus] went ashore he saw a great crowd, and he had compassion on them, because they were like sheep without a shepherd. And he began to teach them many things.

Mark 6:34

Come, let us bow down in worship, let us kneel before the LORD our Maker; for he is our God and we are the people of his pasture, the flock under his care.

Psalm 95:6–7 NIV

There is no fear in love. But perfect love drives out fear, because fear has to do with punishment. The one who fears is not made perfect in love.

1 John 4:18 NIV

"Do not fear, for I am with you; do not be dismayed, for I am your God. I will strengthen you and help you; I will uphold you with my righteous right hand."

Isaiah 41:10 NIV

She Laughs at Days to Come

In 1172 Berta of Bernado died, leaving money in her will for the building of a tower. The following year, workers laid the first stones in the foundation of the tower that would become known as the Leaning Tower of Pisa.

The tower was officially completed in 1370, and it has been doing its best to fall over ever since. Over the years many efforts have been undertaken to halt the tower's slow and steady tilt toward the earth. Very few of the attempts helped at all—and some of the efforts made the problem worse! A better solution may have been found . . . and it will cost between $3 and $4.7 million.

So why does the tower lean?

The problem is the soil on which the tower was built. This mixture of sea shells, clay, and shifting sand just doesn't offer a solid foundation for a construction project.

In Matthew 7:24–27, Jesus told a parable about the wise and foolish builders. The latter built his house on shifting sand, like the Leaning Tower of Pisa. When the storms of life came, the house collapsed. The wise builder, however, built his house on the rock. The storms of life came his way, too, but his house stood firm.

Jesus was very direct about the parable's message: the person who hears His words but fails to put them into practice is like the man who built his house on the shifting sand. Collapse is inevitable, just as life's storms are.

All of us wonder at one time or another if we have what it takes to endure life's storms. I don't know about you, but I want the peace that comes from sinking my roots deep into the truth of Christ and laying the foundation of my life on that Rock! I want to live my life in the peace and security of God's love. Then I can face the future fearlessly, like the woman from Proverbs 31: "She is clothed with strength and dignity; she can laugh at the days to come" (v. 25 NIV).

Resting in the peace of Christ, I too will laugh at the days to come. I hope you'll join me.

> *Lean on . . . stand on . . . build your*
> *life on the One who never moves.*

✺ Five Minutes in the Word ✺

*I am convinced that neither death nor life, neither angels nor
demons, neither the present nor the future, nor any powers, neither
height nor depth, nor anything else in all creation, will be able to
separate us from the love of God that is in Christ Jesus our Lord.*
Romans 8:38–39 NIV

*Consider the blameless, observe the upright; a
future awaits those who seek peace.*
Psalm 37:37 NIV

*When the storms of life come, the wicked are whirled
away, but the godly have a lasting foundation.*
Proverbs 10:25 NLT

*Trust in the LORD with all your heart and do not lean on
your own understanding. In all your ways acknowledge
Him, and He will make your paths straight.*
Proverbs 3:5–6 NASB

Trust in the LORD forever, for the LORD GOD is an everlasting rock.
Isaiah 26:4

Notes

1. Scott Pelley, "Family Members to Alleged Gunman: 'I Forgive You.'" CBS Evening News, June 19, 2015, http://www.cbsnews.com/news/families-show-forgiveness-for-alleged-church-shooter/.

2. Thomas Cahill, *How the Irish Saved Civilization* (New York: First Anchor Books, 1995), 102.

3. Ed Mazza, "A Five-Year-Old Boy Met a Homeless Man for the First Time. What He Did Next Will Bring Tears to Your Eyes," *Huffington Post*, last modified May 19, 2015, http://www.huffingtonpost.com/2015/05/18/waffle-house-homeless_n_7310482.html.

4. Brother Lawrence, *The Brother Lawrence Collection: Practice and the Presence of God, Spiritual Maxims, the Life of Brother Lawrence* (Radford, VA: Wilder Publications), 8.

5. Zac Beauchamp, "Read the Extraordinary Letter Kayla Jean Mueller Sent Her Family Before Her Death," *Vox World*, last modified February 10, 2015, http://www.vox.com/2015/2/10/8012881/kayla-mueller-letter.

6. Herb Boyd, *Autobiography of a People* (New York: Anchor Books, 2000), 44–46.

7. Maurice H. Harris, ed., *Hebraic Literature: Translations from the Talmud, Midrashim, and Kabbala* (New York: Tudor Publishing, 1943).

8. Liz Kreutz, "Charleston Shooting: Mourners Gather for Prayer Service at Morris Brown AME Church," ABC News, last modified June 18, 2015, http://abcnews.go.com/US/charleston-shooting-mourners-gather -prayer-service-morris-brown/story?id=31855986.

9. Eric Metaxas, *Bonhoeffer: Pastor, Martyr, Prophet, Spy* (Nashville, TN: Thomas Nelson, 2011), 153.

10. "Iraqi Christians in Peril," Faith Matters, YouTube, last modified February 5, 2013, https://www.youtube.com/watch?v=YdWMIZU4gsA.

11. Kenneth Bailey, *Jesus Through Middle Eastern Eyes* (Downers Grove, IL: InterVarsity, 2008), 121.

12. Oswald Chambers, *Christian Discipline*, vol. 2 (Crewe UK, CW: Oswald Chambers Publications Association, 1936).

13. Eugene H. Peterson, *Christ Plays in Ten Thousand Places: A Conversation in Spiritual Theology* (Grand Rapids, MI: Eerdmans, 2008), 116.

14. "Believers Burst into Tears and Sing a Beautiful Hymn as Church Cross Is Removed," International Christian Concern, YouTube, last modified June 25, 2014, https://youtube/-pqOrW5JvrQ.

15. *Unbroken*, directed by Angelina Jolie (2014; Universal Pictures), film.

16. Laura Hillenbrand, *Unbroken* (New York: Random House, 2014).

17. Clayborne Carson, *Autobiography of a People* (New York: Grand Central Publishing, 2001), 77.

18 *The Perfect Storm*, directed by Wolfgang Petersen (2000; Warner Brothers), film.

19. Robert J. Morgan, *On This Day* (Nashville: Thomas Nelson, 1997), April 11.

20. Ibid., September 24.

21. Robert J. Morgan, *From This Verse* (Nashville: Thomas Nelson, 1998), December 4.

Want to take 5 more?

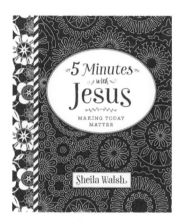

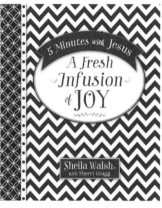

Available now   Available September 2016

Visit 5MinutesWithJesus.com to view
exclusive content and share inspiration!

Connect:

 Facebook.com/5MinWithJesus

 @5MinWithJesus

 @5MinWithJesus